Let There Be Life!

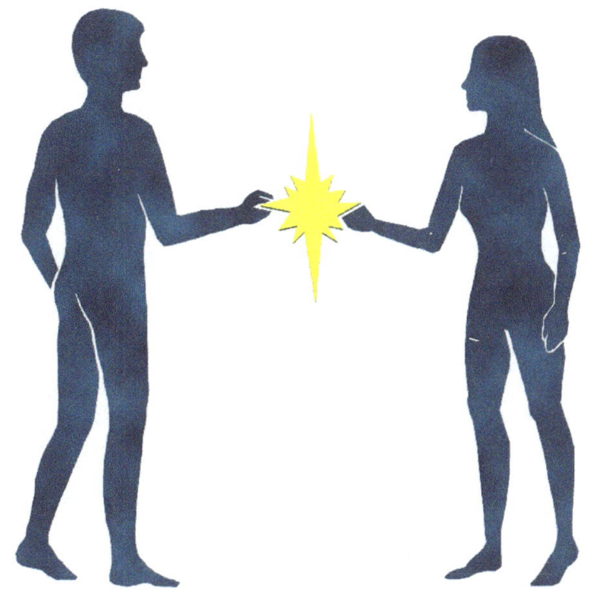

Christopher Alan Anderson

Let There Be Life!

ISBN 978-1506-915-37-1 PBK
ISBN 978-1506-915-38-8 EBK

October 2025

Published and Distributed by
First Edition Design Publishing, Inc.
P.O. Box 17646, Sarasota, FL 34276-3217
www.firsteditiondesignpublishing.com

www.manandwomanbalance.com

Preface

Let There Be Life! consists of two writings (*Let There Be Life!* and *the Man and Woman Balance Invitation Package)* written during the years of 2023 – 2024. As these were smaller writings, I thought it best to combine them into a book together. The theme is the same, Man and Woman Balance and what that means metaphysically and historically. We reside in difficult times. Our fundamental structures that have held life together are breaking down. Actually, they have been breaking down for a long time. Better said, they have never been put together such that they can hold in the first place.

I began these writings on Man and Woman Balance in the early 1970s. A poem here, an expanded thought there. In the later 1970s, I was writing in book form, which were attempts to clarify my thought. I began my first published writing in 1980. It was *The Man and Woman Relationship—A New Center for the Universe.* This was self-published in 1985. And so the journey began. Here I am with these last few writings. These incorporate, and can be used for, promotion as well as the fundamental thought of Man and Woman Balance.

There is a degree of overlap in these writings. My first writings consisted primarily of new material. As the years went by, I begin using quotes from these early writings. You will see many quotes in this writing from my early writings. I also quote from other authors—to compare and contrast. If I am quoting from another author, I list the author's name and the book quoted from if I know the title. If I am quoting from one of my own writings, I just list the title. If you see a quote with just the title listed but not the author you can assume the quote is by me.

Christopher Alan Anderson
March 11, 2025

Table of Contents

Let There Be Life!

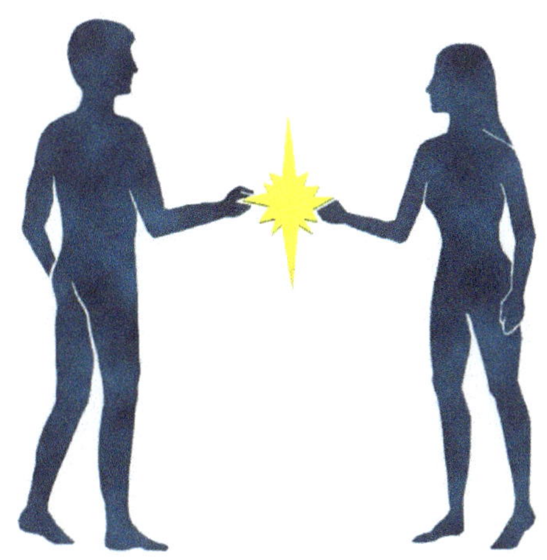

Christopher Alan Anderson
www.manandwomanbalance.com

Preface

Marc and Mark,

Attached is a writing that somewhat exploded out of me these last few weeks. It began as a letter and turned into a treatise.

Two things occurred for me that pushed this on. One was that I am back in contact with First Edition Design Publishing. They are the company that has published all my writings to date. The other was the Opening Ceremonies as the Paris Olympics. Both were a surprise.

Most of this writing concerns the Paris Olympics. The last couple of pages concerns First Edition Design Publishing. But why am I sending this to you two? Because you two, along with Robert and myself, were part of the Russell journey.

I hope you will give some time and thought to this. We are living in very uncertain times. Navigating through this is not easy. I am only here to open a door and I can't do it alone. I need your help as well.

Chris

Let There Be Life!

John 8:32: *And ye shall know the truth, and the truth shall make you free.*

Marc and Mark,*

I am writing to you both because both of you were present and a part of the Walter and Lao Russell journey and I believe connection. Robert,* who we lost last October, was there too.

*Brother Marc, Mark Stanley, swimming buddy, and Robert Birk, college buddy.

Robert presented to me the Glenn Clark book *The Man Who Tapped the Secrets of the Universe* at a swim meet up in Portland. Later, I think it was spring term, 1970, we were able to order most all of the Walter and Lao Russell's writings. I remember the day well when received them. One picture out of one book seemed to mesmerize us both. To this day, I remember just staring at it. Was it hours, days, years; it is still with me.

Walter and Lao Russell—*Atomic Suicide?*, 1957

If you look closely at this picture you will see in this one drawing a paradigm shift, certainly at the spiritual level. The Russell's Divine Trinity certainty is different from the "Holy Trinity" of my upbringing. It alters all of our religions. I didn't know it at the time but this picture became my religion if you will. Later I was to state:

And then Marc, you, Robert and myself attended the 100th birthday celebration in May, 1971 acknowledging Walter Russell and we got to meet Lao Russell and take in Swannanoa and some of Walter Russell's artistic and scientific creations. Lao mentioned to us his opus book, ***The Universal One***, was out of print but that she may bring it back out in the future. And so, on our return home, as we were flying out of Washington D.C., and we had some time before our flight, we went over the Library of Congress and inquired about the book, its current status. And lo and behold, it was out of print and apparently the copyright had expired. Long story short, we were able to have a copy sent to us which came to me in a week or so. I made copies for each of us, you, Mark, Robert, and myself. Now imagine that, we four had a copy of ***The Universal One*** some years before Lao Russell put it back into print. How many other people had

a copy? And Mark, the last time we visited when Marc came out and we went swimming, you said you still had your copy!* Unbelievable!
*Later brother Marc told me he still had his copy!

Well, allow me to share one quote from this great writing.

Walter Russell (1871-1963)—*The Universal One*, 1926

"Sex is of all things from the beginning. Sex begins when light begins. Sex is the desire for the appearance of being which constitutes the appearance of existence. Nothing can be without the desire to be. All things are which desire to be. Desire dominates all thinking. Desire dominates all matter. All desire is sex desire."

Is Dr. Russell suggesting that the motive force of the Universe is of sexual desire? Quite the pill to swallow. I spent years with the Russell's writings including their home study course in ***Universal Law, Natural Science, and Living Philosophy.*** I also have spent years, some fifty or so, looking into this question—A *sexual universe,* the whole of the universe is but a sexual process? This would suggest that each of us exist as sexual beings through a sexual process or interchange. Are we talking male and female here? Apparently so! And moreover, we are speaking of PROCREATION! Many years back I was listening to a talk by Lao Russell which I had acquired on cassette tape. I remember so well; she was speaking to this issue. Suddenly she blurted out, *"Everybody knows it takes a man and a woman to make a baby."* It appears that each of us exist as sexual beings, male or female, part and parcel of a sexual relationship, i.e., male <u>and</u> female. As I often have quoted, *One is not without the other, both are needed for either to be.* Like breathing, inhalation and exhalation. Each part is necessary yet without the other part the whole thing collapses. This suggests that both parts are equally necessary yet they are different/opposite of the other. <u>Equal and Opposite</u>;* we, man and woman, need each other as much as we need ourselves.

*Walter Russell, in his chart of the Periodic Table of the Elements, suggested every element of matter has its polar opposite. For example, sodium and chlorine. He presented to us the idea that sexual difference runs through all things, a Sexual Universe.

Many years ago, Robert sent me a letter/e-mail.

Chris 11/8/99

"In your writings, you have defined the TRUE nature of the WORD as being PROCREATIVE and the ONE order, context, process, and structure of the universe, and that MAN and WOMAN are its TWO electrodes of manifesting! Without you having made this connection from the Russell's, I wouldn't be writing all this down, and there would be no Ruchell and me, and there would be no "The Secret of Creating the Present Moment." The great awakening would still be floundering, waiting for greater definition. This is the second coming as it were. In the name of Ruchell and me, I PROCLAIM it so."

Robert always had a flare to his writing. Unfortunately, due to his illness, he was not able to accomplish much of what he aspired to.

My writings are not so different than that of Alan Watts—*The Two Hands of God*. He was quite the guy back in the day. He was speaking of a polarity, a yin and yang principle or balance which is referenced in the Tao in Eastern thought. This quote is actually from another of his writings.

Alan Watts (1915-1973)—*Tao: The Watercourse Way*, 1975

"The *yin-yang* principle is not, therefore, what we would ordinarily call a dualism, but rather an explicit duality expressing an implicit unity."

Not just a duality of two separate parts nor even a unity of no parts, but a duality and unity interconnected, working together! Jesus speaks of this same thing in the Bible:

Matthew 19:4-6: *Have ye not read, that he which made them in the beginning made them male and female, And said, for this cause shall a man leave father and mother, and shall cleave to his wife: and they twain shall be one flesh?*

> *Wherefore they are no more twain, but one flesh. What therefore God hath joined together, let not man put asunder.*

One of my first insights was that of a ***Two Forces of Creation***.* Here is a quote from that writing which was first published in 1988:

*Titles listed without an author named are from my writings; I am the author.

> **The Two Forces of Creation © 1988—Selected Writings, Volume 2 © 1991, 2010**
>
> In review, let me suggest that "what is," is relationship-in-process. Relationship-in-process is fundamental or primordial, not a First Cause or One Force. This is to further say that there isn't a supreme being although there may be supreme beings. There isn't a mover of the spheres although there may be movers of the spheres. There isn't a one God who sees all that becomes or forms all immortal beings although there may be gods that do just that.* There is not a single fundamental primordial creative force in the universe, i.e., energy, desire, motive, impulse, purpose, impetus, drive, intention, nature, will, consciousness. Prana, mana, Ki. Chi, Waken, bioplasma, light, cosmic energy, life force, vital pulse, or Holy Spirit. There is only one force in relationship to another force from which creation may then occur. We have to date made a critical mistake in not noting this elementary fact within our conception of order.
>
> *Some language taken from the early Greek philosopher Pythagoras, 570-500 B.C.

Two forces, equal and opposite, interconnected and working together, a division of the One and a unity of the Two, that is the universal frame I am presenting, a **procreant** universe. — Life, in a two-way process that cannot be created or destroyed. It just is, alive and procreating, i.e. the **Metaphysical Given** if you will. This brings us to that immense statement/question which Heidegger articulated, and others, too, have asked in different ways:

Martin Heidegger (1888-1976)—German philosopher
"The mystery is that there is something rather than nothing."

Indeed, and I am beginning from the something called Life:

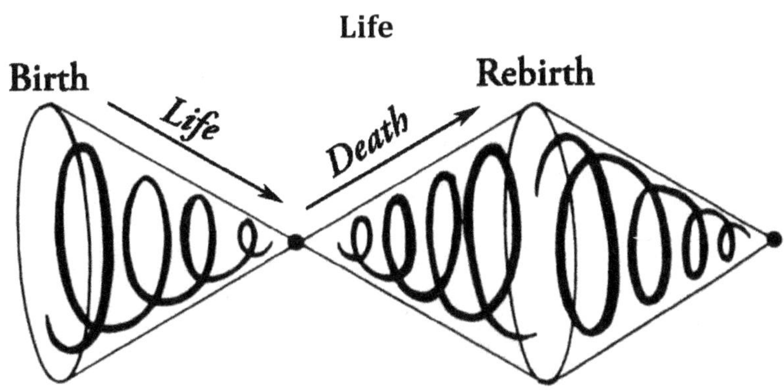

And check this out from Walt Whitman.

Walt Whitman (1819-1892)—*Leaves of Grass,* 1855
"...Urge and urge and urge, Always the procreant urge of the world. Out of the dimness opposite equals advance..."

I have only found this wording in one place and that was in his *Leaves of Grass!*

But there is still another question to ask, and that is: What is the creative purpose/function of Male? and what is the creative purpose/function of Female? Perhaps this is the **Great Abstraction**. Matt Walsh of the Daily Wire asked the question, "What is a woman?" and it went around the globe. But must not we also ask, "What is a man?" We really can't know one without the other. So as not to make a book out of this letter let me give you the short answer—which is not so short. This is also from **The Two Forces of Creation.**

Male is that force which seeks to individualize form separate and apart from the unity of male-female. The male desire is to hold male and female in individual form. It is the active *conscious* effort of holding separate identity in relationship to the other. The male effort is simply to hold apart and stabilize the man and woman relationship. We call this the effort to secure form or just *security.*

Female is that force which seeks to unite the division of male and female. The female desire is to unite the separate male and female forms together as one. She rests the man and woman relationship through unifying male within herself. It is from this unity that the next division or reproduction can take place. The female effort then is to unite the separate forms of male and female, resting that unity so that the next reproduction of individual form will occur. We call this resting of old form/begetting of new form *reproduction.*

In essence, it is the male effort to secure form and the female effort to reproduce form that makes for life and its continuity. Each aspect makes for one half of the creative process. Yet, and this is an important point, neither aspect can complete their creative desire without the other. The male cannot continually secure form. That effort is fatiguing and brings on a desire to rest. It is at this point that the male takes what he has secured in form and gives it over to female. The male deposits his life seed (force) into the female releasing his form into hers from which his next reproduction will occur. So without periodic rest or release of his form into hers, the male cannot continue to fulfill his own desire to secure form.

Likewise, the female cannot continually rest/reproduce form. She herself must sequentially effort, and does so equal to male in preparing herself to receive male as well as nurturing new form. In this fashion, she supports the securing effort of male. Female is actually called to surrender her life to the male desire to individualize form even though her primary desire is to unite, for without that division of the one into two there would not be the two sexual selves to unite. At this point of unity, the male is called to surrender his life to the female desire to unite the forms even though his primary desire is to individualize. Without the unity of the two into one there would not be a unified one from which male and female could then divide into their sexually unique forms.

It is important to understand the equality of the two different forces of male and female. They each operate under different desires and yet both are equally essential for either of them to be. The male force alone or the female force alone is impotent. Without the other neither can be. They *need* each other. Each is as important to the other as they are to themselves. Both are called upon to make the ultimate surrender of their lives to the other. Neither is ever without the other. Both always are. Male and female, the two forces of creation, are what is. We might just say:

Male, being that force which seeks to individualize a form separate and apart from the unity of male-female.

Female, being that force which seeks to unite separate forms together from the division of male and female.

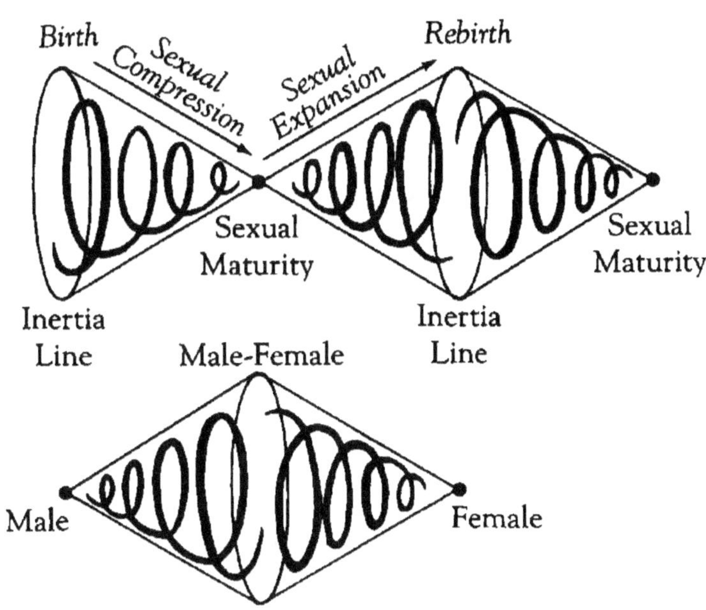

And from some of my other writings:

The Discovery of Life © 1994, 2010

We express creation through our sexuality. That is the effort of individual life. Then we release our sexual difference into the unity of rest. In the unification of the two, sexual difference, in that one moment, is voided. The two have become one which is their rest or death. But from that unity comes the next division into sexual difference. This whole process is sexual, creative to life. (I hope it is understood that sexuality is not just physical but metaphysical. It is of the non-beginning and never-ending. It is what is. In other words, we are not beings who just happen to be sexual, we are sexual beings with a sexual purpose.) So, which do you do? Do you divide the one or do you unite the two? This is the great metaphysical question. To answer it, we need to discover our sexual selves, who we are in relation to whom we are not, thereby discovering life. If you are a male, you will do one of these functions. If you are a female, you will do the other. Both functions are equally necessary to life, yet they are opposite. So which are you?

The Metaphysics of Sex...In a Changing World © 2014

On a personal note, when Mr. Anderson was asked to describe the writings and what he felt their message was he responded, "Spiritual procreation. Mankind has yet to distinguish the two sexes on the spiritual level. In this failure lies the root of our problems and why we cannot yet touch the eternal together. The message of Man and Woman Balance brings each of us together in love with our eternal other half right now."

The Eternal Marriage from **Man, Woman, and God © 1994, 2010**

The spiritual connection is a connection between a man and a woman whereby they recognize their eternal creation and love together. It is based in their sexual differentiation from and creative need for each other. In this, a man and woman have *life* purpose together. They are the co-creators of all that is. The formed universe moves through them. They together hold the balance on which all life depends. The world moves one step forward into the light with just one touch of their love.

So why am I conveying this to you at this time? One of the reasons is the Paris Olympics. Did you see the Opening Ceremonies?

> PARIS (AP) — Paris: The Olympic gold medalist of naughtiness.
>
> Revolution ran like a high-voltage wire through the wacky, wonderful and rule-breaking Olympic opening ceremony that the French capital used to astound, bemuse and, at times, poke a finger in the eye of global audiences on Friday night.
>
> That Paris put on the most flamboyant, diversity-celebrating, LGBTQ+-visible of opening ceremonies wasn't a surprise. Anything less would have seemed a betrayal of the pride the French capital takes in being a home to humanity in all its richness.
>
> But still. Wow. Paris didn't just push the envelope. It did away with it entirely as it hammered home a message that freedom must know no bounds.
>
> A practically naked singer painted blue made thinly veiled references to his body parts. Blonde-bearded drag queen Piche crawled on all fours to the thumping beat of "Freed From Desire" by singer-songwriter Gala, who has long been a potent voice against homophobia. There were the beginnings of a menage à trois—the door was slammed on the camera before things got really steamy—and the tail end of an intimate embrace between two men who danced away, hugging and holding hands.

Did you hear this, *"Paris didn't just push the envelope. It did away with it entirely as it hammered home a message that freedom must know no bounds."* It's almost like they were just giving us the middle finger. Think about it, this Opening Ceremony had to be planned out and approved by the International Olympic Committee not to mention at high levels of the French government. Makes one wonder, for what purpose? To me, this was demonic, and that is deeply disturbing. In a way though it brings to light the critical issue/question: Is this a universe of no bounds or is it one of absolute bounds? That is to say, is there a fundamental order to things or is there not? I guess you know which side I stand on and have been writing about all these years. Do you, or anyone, believe that LIFE is or can be contained in the no bounds, anything goes criterion as presented by the LGBTQ movement? (Q means queer which means no boundaries.) And you know what, they are going after the children, just look at the Trans movement. Or perhaps there are exact bounds, absolute bounds to LIFE like the Two Force (Equal and Opposite) frame of Man and Woman Balance, the only frame that is procreative to LIFE? *"Everybody knows it takes a man and a woman to make a baby."* Well, I guess everybody doesn't know.

Let me ask, if someone has a "sexual" orgasm watching Cowboys and Indians on TV, is that sex? We would call that fantasy, would we not? If someone has a "sexual" orgasm playing/touching a naked child, is that sex? No, we call that child abuse. We seem to call anything, such as sodomy, sex if it gets one off. Sodomy is not a sexual act; it is a deviation from the sexual act. Even Freud in his writing *The Sexual Life of Human Beings*, 1920, stated: "*The abandonment of the reproductive function is the common feature of all perversions.*" Sex, or the sexual act, is geared to the unification of a man and a woman. Only opposites can unite. And what is the big deal about sexual unification. That is what brings forth the next division of life, i.e. procreation. Not all sexual acts result in the procreation of a baby boy or baby girl. But there is a spiritual component going on as well, that man and woman have united from which they will again divide. Let us return to Walt Whitman.

Walt Whitman (1819-1892)—*Leaves of Grass: I Sing the Body Electric*, 1855

> "This is the nucleus…after the child is born of woman the man is born of woman. This is the bath of birth…this is the merge of small and large and the outlet again."

Sexual acts can only take place between a man and a woman, equal and opposite. Sex only exists within the parameter of male and female. The further we get away of this reality the harder we fall.

Elon Musk, in a recent talk* with Jordan Peterson, spoke of the loss of his son due to puberty blockers and Woke Culture. It is as if his Son has died, not literally, but is forever gone from him. That's got to hurt. "So, I vowed to destroy the Woke mind virus after that," he stated. And, moreover, how wrong we are if we don't embrace the

LGBTQ agenda. How misguided and even cruel we are if we speak out for LIFE. I guess "tolerance" is only to run one way.

*Red State, 7/24/24

The Woke (DEI) Culture just keeps coming at you. Some years back San Francisco Chronicle reported that a California state senator was attempting to resurrect a bill "...that would allow voluntary intercourse between teenagers between the ages of 14 to 17 and with adults who are less than 10 years older. Intercourse, in this case, would expand to include anal or oral sex, or vaginal penetration with anything other than a penis." The point being is that they keep pushing the envelope, undoubtedly for that day when man/boy "love" is legal and celebrated.

Also, here in California there is the "Safety Act" that forbids teachers or school staff into notify parents if a child changes their gender identity or pronouns. Could this become Federal Law? I am sure some politicos are pushing it. And the parents have no say, and don't even get to know! When did the State become the owners of the children?

Just this last week I heard a bill* had passed in the Massachusetts House and Senate that "replaces the traditional terms "Father" and "Mother" on birth certificates with the terms "person who gave birth" and "other parent." It is now awaiting the governor's signature."

*Reported by Republic Nation 8/7/24

Today I hear* that Dr. Jordan B Peterson lost his appeal to the High (Supreme) Court of Canada. He states, "The court has rejected my appeal regarding the decision of the Ontario Collage of Psychologists to subject me to indefinite re-education...primarily for publicly opposing the 'butchers and liars subjecting children to sterilization and mutilation....' I am also required to pay whatever court costs the Collage accrued in relation to my appeal.... I am now bereft of options on the legal front in Canada."

*Reported in RedState, 8/9/24

You may have heard of Riley Gaines*, the collegiate swimmer, from a few years back. She, and her whole University of Kentucky Swim Team, was told to "stand down, clamp it, and take it" regarding a "transgender" swimmer, not just swimming again her but using the girl's locker room facilities as well. What happened to Title IV, the Woman's Protection Act?

*If not, check out *Swimming Against the Current* with Mike Rowe*: Riley Gaines Hates Losing More Than She Loves Winning* on YouTube. If that does not drive this issue home, I don't know what will.

This is the issue, my issue, that Life is contained in the perfect equal and opposite balance between male and female—and lives! The whole LGBTQ movement seems to be about non-life—two men or two women are not procreative to Life. And we can't even speak up! **Luke23:34:** *"Father, forgive them; for they know not what they do."* And you know what, if one's core belief system is imbalanced going in so will one's actions be imbalanced toward others going out. This is the crucial point. It sounds so nice to say, *Live and let live.* Easier said than done when some are proclaiming *Love is love* and, at the same time, advocating for parents to have little to no say in the education of their children.

What we can learn from this? Is it that every child needs a Father and a Mother? *If there is a God the Father there must also be a God the Mother....* Every child needs family. But family is not to be defined by anyone's discretion, is it? Interesting that in Marx and Engels' Communist Manifesto there was the call for the dissolution of the (man and woman two-parent) family. Did they know that one's fundamental loyalty, stronger then even (socialist) government, was to family? Family doesn't have to be forced upon us; it lives within us. And so, family had to be broken for the real communist takeover to occur. And isn't this what is happening with the LGBTQ phenomena? "Love is love" and "Can't we all just live together" turns out to be "We are coming after your children," the children they can't conceive as the acts of sodomy and the use of strap-ons, etc., are not procreative to life. I apologize for having to use those terms but A is A; those acts cannot be expressions of love or life. They comprise a category mistake/metaphysical fraud where somehow A is B and B is A. It's like we are living an Orwellian nightmare where everything *"is designed to make lies sound truthful and sexual depravity* respectable."* What is next, a Gay Manifesto? Oh, that has already been written!** Listen to these words:

> "We shall sodomize your sons, emblems of your feeble masculinity, of your shallow dreams and vulgar lies. We shall

seduce them in your schools, in your dormitories, in your gymnasiums, in your locker rooms, in your sports arenas, in your seminaries, in your youth groups, in your movie theater bathrooms, in your army bunkhouses, in your truck stops, in your all male clubs, in your houses of Congress, wherever men are with men together...

"There will be no compromises. We are not middle-class weaklings. Highly intelligent, we are the natural aristocrats of the human race, and steely-minded aristocrats never settle for less. Those who oppose us will be exiled...

"The family unit-spawning ground of lies, betrayals, mediocrity, hypocrisy and violence—will be abolished. The family unit, which only dampens imagination and curbs free will, must be eliminated.

"We shall be victorious because we are fueled with the ferocious bitterness of the oppressed who have been forced to play seemingly bit parts in your dumb, heterosexual shows throughout the ages. We too are capable of firing guns and manning the barricades of the ultimate revolution...."

*Orwell used the word 'murder' in his quote. I changed it to 'sexual depravity'.

***Homosexual Manifesto* (also called *Gay Revolutionary)* by Michael Swift, 1987. This was actually read into the Congressional record.

And this is only a few paragraphs from the document. Makes one wonder, what is next? How about changing the purpose of Grammer school from reading, writing, and arithmetic to being *"The time for children to choose their own gender"?* It's the family they are after. They want to destroy the man, woman, and child family. Isn't that clear to all? We can't separate life and love from its procreative foundation, can we? The answer to LGBTQ ought not to be a Celebration* of that "Lifestyle" but a healing of the heart and soul within. Let us love ye one another but at the same time not condone what is contrary to life itself. And we can begin with recognizing Marriage as between <u>one man and one woman</u>, as that is the union which is procreative life.

*Why do we have a whole month (June) to celebrate LGBTQ and only one day to celebrate Mother's Day or Father's Day?

We Can Only Create Together

- Man and woman can only create together.
- From the love of a man and a woman new life, a son or a daughter, is born.
- All new born life is divine life.
- Each creation is a divine creation.
- Each creation is the most special creation.
- Each creation is bequeathed with the divine love of Father and Mother.
- Every creation has within its heart the desire to create life with and through its other half.
- Every creation is eternal in its procreative balance with its eternal other half.
- The heartbeat within every creation is the heartbeat of procreative love.
- Procreative love is the life-dynamic of the universe.
- Procreative love is God.
- God is Man and Woman Balance.
- God is expressed when a man and a woman reach out to each other and touch in the one pure, perfect moment of their most special love.
- Only together can a man and a woman create.

Some believe Christianity will step in and somehow save the day. Perhaps, but Christianity has its own faults, such as a hierarchical priesthood and the singular Jesus as the only savior. I would rather suggest that Christianity is really about a touch. *"Who touched me?"* (Mark 5:31) It is not so much an intellectual understanding but a touch of two hearts. *...believe with one's heart.* (Romans 10:9) As Robert stated *"In your writings, you have defined the TRUE nature of the WORD as being PROCREATIVE and the ONE order, context, process, and structure of the universe, and that MAN and WOMAN are its TWO electrodes of manifesting!"* Let us ask, can "God" create, or Life be, something other than Man and Woman? **Genesis 1:27:** *So God created man in his own image, in the image of God created he him, male and female created he them.* There is no other creation for the ***Spirit of God*** is the ***Spirit of Life*** is the ***Spirit of Man and Woman Balance*** ! Man and Woman Balance is ***Love***, and a child is born! This is not hierarchical. Nor is it limited just to Jesus. We are all an only begotten Son or an only begotten Daughter, not singularly but in relationship together!

Unfortunately, Christianity, as currently structured, cannot stop the LGBTQ onslaught as it, Christianity, failed to make the sexual (two-force) distinction on the metaphysical/spiritual level of things. Where is procreation a priori? (If there is a God the Father there must be a God the Mother...) Look at how many Christian denominations are embracing the LGBTQ agenda! This cannot work. It can only fail. Someone must say ENOUGH! Marc, our Father* said ENOUGH to the IRS. I will say ENOUGH to LGBTQ!

*Stanley Anderson, in the 1990s, audited by the IRS, said ENOUGH! Six years of hell. Thankfully, with the assistance of Ronald Peter MacDonald, he was able to prevail.

And if you think what I have thus far presented is bad, take in the quote from the writing below of which Ron MacDonald was a co-author. This quote is on a different subject, but in a way the two go together and support each other.

Ronald P. MacDonald and Robert Rowen, M.D.—*They Own It All (Including You!) By Means of Toxic Currency,* 2009

"With the veil of deceit lifted, you have now discovered that you don't own anything. You are using another entity's property in all your contracts. The foundation of liberty is the ownership of property. Without property that is exclusively yours, how can you enter into any sort of contract without the permission of the lien holder? Simply put, you can't.

"Furthermore, your use of FRNs identifies you as a debtor in use of the creditor's property. You, and every contract into which you enter with its property, are subject to its terms and conditions.

"...Within a few years of the gold confiscation and replacement by marked debt notes, came laws of the kind never seen before in America. Roosevelt's New Deal, allegedly for recovery of the Depression, created agency after agency, board after board, license after license. Occupations, which are your common law right to work, suddenly required a license. A license is permission by the state to do that which otherwise would be illegal.

"...How did even marriage come to need state permission by license? Previously it was a holy contract entered into before God in a house of worship. How did the spiritual product of this union, children, need registration with the state? The answer is that we have become the chattel property of some entity (the Federal Reserve Bank), requiring registration and permission.

"...In 1933, the U.S. government went insolvent. It too then became a debtor subject to the creditor. But you weren't told. We the People don't have any idea what the terms and conditions of that Chapter 11 bankruptcy included. But the evidence leaves a clear trail. The government became the agent of collection for the creditor. The debt was dumped on us. We were collectively beguiled into a debtor's status. The creditor worked the terms and conditions through the government. If the creditor did this openly, we would not be beguiled. But the cruelest and most unconscionable effect from this act is that it is perpetual!"

"It is perpetual!" Scary words. Do you understand that our "money" is but a debt/loan. You do not own the money in your wallet. You are borrowing it from a foreign entity called the Federal Reserve System and you must pay it back with interest. And our politicos borrow and borrow like drunken sailors. When was the last time they balanced a budget? You and I and the American people right today owe some 10, or is it 100, trillion dollars. This is not sustainable. The dollar is but a debt dollar. It's the debt of the Washington D. C. (U.S.) corporation. And where did the Washington D. C. (U.S.) corporation get the power to spend money they did not have? They stole it by placing **We the People** under their jurisdiction without our knowing it. *"The government became the agent of collection for the creditor. The debt was dumped on us. We were collectively beguiled into a debtor's status."* Think of the IRS. The income tax was never to be placed on the (sovereign) individual. It was to be a corporate tax, and rightly so. **We the People** are the sovereign, with unalienable rights! Corporations are creations of the government. Corporations have way too much power today. One could argue that they are running our government/politicos. Corporate autocracy! I suggest we disallow corporations from funding those running for office. And get the income tax off the back of individuals.

We must return to a sound money system of value, i.e., gold and silver, for example, such that each one of us has allodial/absolute title to our money. Again, this debt is not really the people's debt. Moreover, the dollar is crashing as we speak. Countries around the world are abandoning dollar*, and rightly so. We can't be a sovereign on a debt/loan system. Our *Declaration of Independence* and *Constitution for the United States of America* mean nothing if we do not have absolute ownership to the money in our wallets and purses (bank accounts etc.). There are signs that things are moving in this direction. Until then, we are living under a fake money system that can rightly be called the Poverty Hoax.

*After World War II the Bretton Woods Agreement was put into place creating the International Monetary Fund (IMF) and the International Bank for Reconstruction and Development, also known as the World Bank. If that system worked at all it worked only as long as the dollar was pegged to gold. That ended in 1971.

The Man and Woman Manifesto: Let the Revolution Begin © 1994, 2010

Everything dies within the poverty hoax. Business dies, relationship and family die, love dies, the spirits of men and women die. We see the end result of poverty, despair, violence, and death all around us. People are being used up, lives wasted, businesses lost. And many people sense something is wrong. The church leaders speak up and tell us we need to be more compassionate and forgiving. The state rulers claim we need to sacrifice one more time. Yet, no one speaks of economic freedom, the only doorway to success and prosperity. *Economic freedom gives to us universal independence, opening the door to create value and do business anywhere in the universe.*

As a side note, something that would greatly help in giving to money its proper backing is energy. Money is frozen energy if you will. We are now on a carbon-based system of energy, coal and oil, of diminishing returns. Also, there is nuclear power. It has a waste disposal problem. Remember what Walter Russell said about nuclear power.

Walter and Lao Russell—*Atomic Suicide?,* 1957

"Radiation is the normal death principle. Everything in Nature dies normally by slowly radiating its heat. Radioactivity is the explosively quick death principle. Radioactivity is man's discovery of how the human race can die quickly, and not be able to propagate its kind for many long centuries.

"...All things in Nature die normally by slow expansion. Radioactivity is multiplied expansion, which is caused by multiplied compression. It helps man die from explosively quick expansion. Flame is caused by maximum compression. Flame is the ultimate consumer of all bodies."

If we could only tap into the ether energy, also called free energy or zero-point energy as Nikola Testa and Walter Russell* sought. But there isn't any money to be made in "Free Energy," the small minds complain. But would not that bring stability and honesty to the money system, not to mention break the strangle hold rich countries have on poorer counters? The politicos and robber barons would not be able to pad their pockets! The debt dollar is directly linked to the diminishing returns/damage (debt) of our current energy systems.

*Ether Energy from Walter's Russell's Optic Dynamo-Generator—Energy in the 9 Octaves Model Manifest, You Tube.

So, let's see how their game is played? It is simple. They, the politicos, also called insiders, the Deep Staters, the never be fired bureaucrats, the war hawk neocons, etc. create a problem to which they then come marching in as if they are our saviors. Certainly, we can't complain if they spend a billion (or is it a trillion) of our "tax dollars" in "solving" the problem, can we?. And, of course, they, the politicos, get to pad their own pockets which was their real motive all along! Let me take one example. 911. Look at the mileage they, the government, got out of that disaster. A whole new agency was created, Homeland Security, with a billion + dollar budget. A war was justified, the Iraq war. (I thought the planes were flown by Saudi pilots!) And what about that missile hitting the Pentagon? Oh, and why did Building 7 collapse hours later when it was never hit? This whole thing doesn't past the smell test. Neither does COVID 19. Look how we accepted the COVID 19 vaccine without ever asking, *what is in it*! (How dare to even ask!) Then we were told to "shelter in place." Does that go for the homeless as well? Notice how Big Pharma, with the help of Big Government and Big Media, shunned anyone who dared to question their narrative or suggest another remedy that was outside of their control and profit. Day-by-day it is now being revealed that COVID 19 was more of a con, a power grab for control and money.* And let's not forget the World Health Organization who is seeking world domination over each country's health policies as we speak.

*See the Kingston Report, Karen Kingston

And it goes on and on. How about the Ukraine war? Who is funding it? Hundreds of billions spent. Hundreds of thousands dead. The country destroyed. That is a NATO/Washington D.C. created war. Robert F. Kennedy Jr., in his speech to the American people on 8/23/24, spoke of created wars, not wars where we have been attacked but wars that the politicos/military industry complex insiders create.* Wow? I have never looked at it that way. "We live in interesting times." Let's change that to read, "We live in uncertain/scary times." Let me ask, who is the President of the United States right now? He seems to be retired! The person who apparently took his place has been nominated but not yet elected? So, who is holding the nuclear codes? This is scary.

*Let's give deep thanks for those in the military who still believe and stand for We the People and the true values thereof.

How about the open boarder? Thousands and thousands of undocumented people, mostly males, streaming across it every day. Is there a purpose to this? (See what is happening in the UK at this very moment. We are probably six months or so out from that happening here.) How about election fraud? Apparently, we can't even have an election that has independent oversight? Why? Because they, the Deep State politicos, have to cheat to win. How do I know this? Because they advocate a "right to vote" for people who are not even citizens of this country. And if the Deep State players see that they can't win they just may try to postpone the election or, even worse, attempt to create a civil war. Another reason why illegals are streaming across our boarder?

Robert F. Kennedy Jr. also spoke about how sick the American people are, especially the children. Obesity, diabetes, heart disease, cancer, autism, psychotic breaks, etc. Might there be a connection here with all the dead foods we consume, foods full of pesticides, dyes, and sugar? And what about the chemtrails? Does anyone know what is really going on? Or the number of vaccines children are given today? Or how about the psychotropic drugs? Or how about abortion on demand. Certainly, the LGBTQ crowd favors no restrictions—*...that freedom must know no bounds.* But isn't life sacred even when it is in a mother's tummy?* ISN'T LIFE SACRED! Man and Woman Balance says YES! Instead, we have the Paris Opening Ceremonies shoved right in our faces. Well, if the Paris Opening Ceremonies showed us anything it is that we are at the time where we must stand up to this destructive LGBTQ mind virus and call it for what it is, not so much by standing against it (resistance/violence) but by standing for Man and Woman Balance (acceptance of Life/procreant love). If we don't, one day we may all be facing some type of experience as Elon Musk, Jordan Peterson, Riley Gaines, and so many others have had to face. Let us *"Think on these things."* **Philippians 4:8** What is your ENOUGH point? Is it going to be Man and Woman Balance = natural Law = The Sanctity of Life = The Bill of Rights = Common Law = The 1st Amendment = The 2nd Amendment = Asset backed currency = Saving the children or is it going to non-Life?

*Let's go back to the Hyde Amendment, 1976, limiting abortion to cases of rape, incest, or life-threatening pregnancies. In the first two cases the woman's (or girl's) choice has been stolen from her. She still retains it. In the last case, her life is at stake. Perhaps she will choose to give birth to and raise the child. Or give birth to and find a family to adopt the child. Hopefully there is a man/husband in her life that will support her through this difficult time.

If we can learn just one thing, let us learn that the dark side of man (male) is predatory. Since day one, he has used and abused woman in any and every way. He has not known or could not comprehend, yet feel within himself, that standing right in front of him, **woman**, was, and is, his <u>eternal savior</u>. His salvation/unity lies <u>only</u> in **woman**. The continuation of his SOUL lies <u>only</u> in **woman**, i.e., PROCREATION. Men, feel it!

The Divine Touch: A New Creation For Life © 2021

"If you do not position the life process (Man and Woman Balance) as the metaphysical primary of life, you will never be able to defend life."

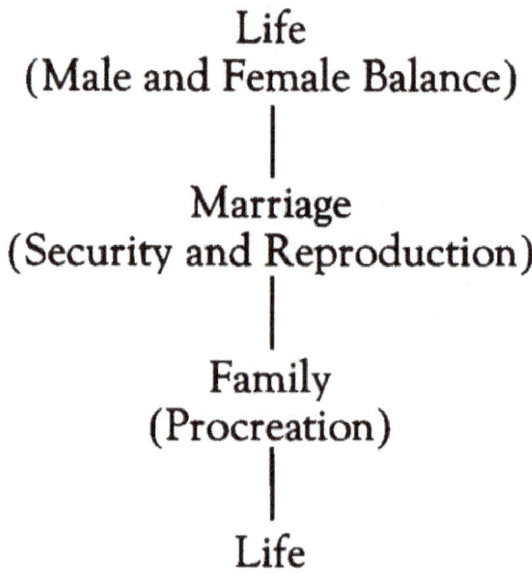

I must say, saying ENOUGH is not so easy. But it is necessary. Do you two remember Craig Larson*? When he first came upon some of my writings he commented, "These are some two-hundred years out."

*Craig Larson lived at the big house, my home at the time, from December 2005 to June, 2015.

The following was written by his friend Jon Hendricks and was read at Craig's memorial service. Marc, you were at Craig's service at the house. Jon Hendricks was there as well.

> ***The loss of friend Craig Larson who changed the world as we know it.***
>
> *Craig, a computer code cracker, broke one of the greatest mystery codes in computer history. It became what is known as a foundation patent that would be integrated into everything. He figured out how to sync audio and video together over a phone line it became known as DSL. The technology was used everywhere and became so big so fast it became impossible for him to ever settle for anything. To me he will be remembered as a great friend who made life style choices he lived by. I am proud and honored to have helped him in pursuit of his dream. His life was not as much about money as it was about his love of technology, music, and people. God rest his wonderful Spirit and his Soul be webcast to the stars and beyond the other side. We love you Craig... Rock on my friend.*

My reply to Craig was "that due to your jump ahead technology the world is instantly synced up; there is only NOW!" Now is the only time to say ENOUGH! From this moment on, there is no going back! Let us hear; let the whole world hear, from this moment on there is no going back!

As a side note to you Marc, I am sure you remember the time you, Craig, and myself attended a Moody Blues* concert at the Luther Burbank Center. This was in April 2015, I believe. At this time the band was missing Michael Pinder. Michael Pinder was one of my favorite Moody Blues' members. His classic song *I'm a Melancholy Man* touched me deeply in my late teens/early twenties. It still touches me deeply; made it okay for me to be somewhat of an introspective loner! The band members were introducing support musicians and lo and behold they introduced Michael Pinder who was in the audience. At intermission, Craig pressed himself over to where Michael Pinder was sitting and introduced us to him. I was able to tell Micheal how his song gave to me LIFE, it touched me so. He had a grin from ear to ear.

The Moody Blues, the Russell's; I could also mention Ayn Rand, Walt Whitman, Thomas Troward, *A Course in Miracles,* and many more, so influential in shaping my metaphysical thought.

Let's return to some further Russell quotes:

Walter and Lao Russell—*Home Study Course in Universal Law, Natural Science, and Living Philosophy,* Unit 6, Lesson 22, 1951

"Mankind has thought of sex in terms of a relation between the opposite sexes in organic living systems, never for a moment including sex relations in the mineral kingdom, in hot suns, or the ice caps of the poles of planets. We have used such terms as cohabitation and sex relation as though the sex relation is entirely separate and apart from other relations, and as though its reproductive effect is limited to living things that die or decay.

"From now on, sex will be regarded in our new perspective as being expressed continuously and perpetually in all things. Instead of thinking in terms of cohabitation and human sexual relationships, sex should be thought of as the interchange between pairs of oppositely unbalanced conditions for the purpose of balancing these conditions in every effect of motion in the entire universe. "Good effects" are those in which the interchange is balanced—and "bad effects" are those in which balance is not complete."

Lao Russell— *Love,* 1966

"Man and woman are forever seeking balanced mates, for they intuitively know that with and through each other they have a greatly multiplied power of expression. The scientific explanation of this multiplied power lies in the fact that not only their bodies but their thinking, also, becomes polarized. This polarization can only come from sex mate-hood between man and woman. That is why homosexuality has a weakening effect rather than a strengthening one. It naturally follows that lesbianism has the same weakening effect. Male and female sex intercourse brings polarization to *balanced* mates. There is a great vitalizing force for both when true love has given birth to the sex desire.

"When a male has sexual relations with another male, or a female with a female, there is not a polarization, but rather a depolarization, which has a *devitalizing* effect. Naturally, the thinking of such people is also unbalanced. In one of our lessons in our *Home Study Course in Universal Law, Natural Science, and Living Philosophy* is the following on POLARITY:

"The basic law of Creation demands equality in all interchange between the pairs of units in all Creation....

"Nature will not tolerate any violation of sex-balance whatsoever and that is why we see anguish, disease, frustrations, divorces, bankruptcies, and many forms of unhappiness around about us everywhere in small scale, and hatreds, enmities, and wars in large scale. All of the troubles of all the world lie in that one cause—breach of the law of polarity which upsets the balance of every transaction between DIVIDED PAIRS.

"When a transaction between divided pairs fails to UNITE those divided pairs, unhappiness is as sure to follow as night follows day. A seesaw is an excellent example of polarity or sex-division. That is why we choose this example. It is important that you realize and recognize that similarity. A seesaw divides the one balance of its fulcrum into two extended balances which must be equally balanced in order to unite and repeat.

"Every interchange is a sex interchange. When a man and woman *talk* together, this is a *mental sex interchange.* Powerful ideas are born of mental sex interchange when a man and woman are *balanced mental mates.* That is why men and women should work together—mentally—

because they would then know the ecstasy of balance mental mate-hood.

"Everyone should know the importance of *balanced mating.* A marriage which is based purely upon physical attraction is not a balanced mating. *There must be a spiritual, mental, and physical harmony to fulfill the electrical balance necessary for balanced mate-hood. There is no law on earth that will hold two people together who do not truly love each other."*

Do you hear the words of Lao Russell? *There must be a spiritual, mental, and physical harmony to fulfill the electrical balance necessary for balanced mate-hood.* Procreation is not just physical; it runs all the way up to the spiritual. To date, this is what we have missed—we failed to distinguish the two sexes on the spiritual level. *Spiritual Procreation, i.e., Man and Woman Balance, is the source/center of Life because it is Life.* LET THERE BE LIFE!

And then there is her wonderful quote from:

Lao Russell (1904-1988)—*Why You Cannot Die: The Continuity of Life,* 1972

"Know thou that thou shalt know space, but never emptiness for:

"Behold! I am Space and I fill all of it.

"I am its One, its undivided Father-Mother One of my universe.

"I divide My oneness, and behold! I am two—father and mother.

"These two extend from Me, one on My right hand and one on My left.

"Each equally balanced with the other in the Oneness of their mate-hood.

"And then, behold! My two become one in Me, the One Father-Mother, undivided—

"To again become two to Father-Mother my eternal universe."

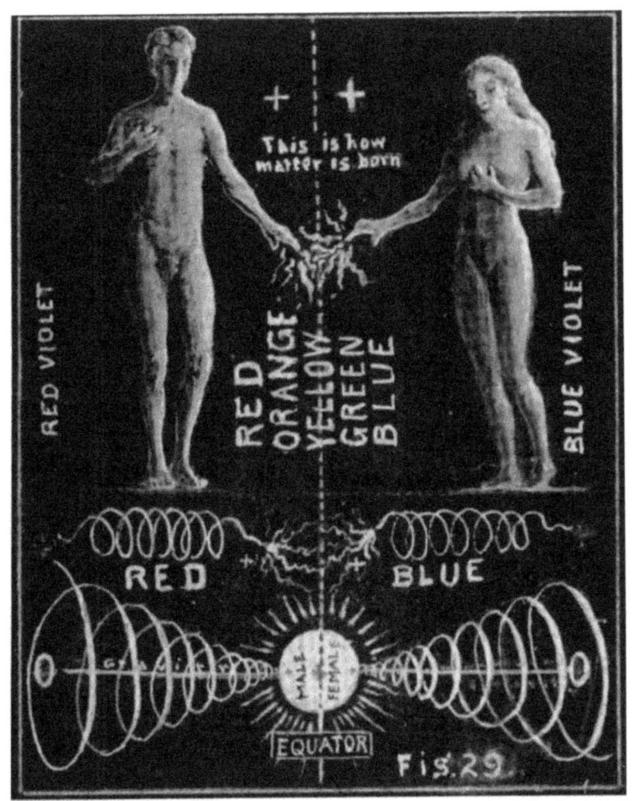

Walter and Lao Russell—*Atomic Suicide?*, 1957

If I may conclude with quotes from my writings:

Meditations for Deepening Love © 1994, 2010
Meditation to Son

My dear Son, you were only just a babe, and now look at you. You have come through the years well; you've grown into your own manhood ready to take on the responsibilities thereof. What more could I ask for? What would make me happier than to see you now in your place in life, securing your life and family? I remember the many esoteric talks we have had over the years while you were struggling over the great questions, seeking to discover the meaning of life. But now they are answered for you, aren't they? Your actions tell me so as you have found the priority of your family. And so I tried to tell you, my son, in my actions. Do you now know why my family always came first with me? But now I am growing old. Things are in your hands now. You lead the world, in your own way. You take your place amongst the great, in your own way. You keep your family together, and through your actions teach your son the meaning of life. And in that thought I will go to my rest, always knowing, always proud, that you are my son.

Meditation to Daughter

My dearest daughter, how could I have ever told you what it means to be a woman? Yes, you thought you knew; at times you were so sure, you would look at me wondering what I knew about life. But now you know, don't you? Yes, my blessed daughter, you, too, have now crossed the channel from woman to mother. You, too, have given birth to a baby, your baby. And now you know; I could see it in your eyes when you first held your baby to your breast. You, my daughter, have brought forth life, just as I had done. And then the look you gave me showing me your understanding, and love, that I am your mother and you are my child, just as you are now the mother of your child. Now you know, my daughter, why I could not explain motherhood in its purpose in my life to you, just as you won't be able to explain it to your daughter. She, too, must first give birth to know herself and her mother. Thank you, my daughter, for now knowing me as your mother and knowing yourself as my daughter.

Let Us Create Life Together from **Meditations for Deepening Love © 1994, 2010**

Suddenly, her heart stirred again. *It is I.* Emotion flooded over the woman's body. "Is this man to take me to the truth?" she asked herself. He was still just sitting there. He had not given any notice to her to confirm. "What shall I do?" she thought.

"I am a *man.* I only know the truth with *woman.* Man and woman *together* are the truth. I seek the woman who seeks me, that we may *create life together."*

"What can I do to help?" she uttered. "We don't want the truth to die." The man responded saying, "The truth lives only as it is *reproduced.* The truth lives only through man and woman. If I have been sent with this message then I must not have been sent alone." The man paused and then trembled as he said, *"May you be the one who has been sent with me. May you be the one to extend beyond me."*

That was her question, her truth. And once more the woman's heart stirred and she spoke the words even before she heard them. *Let us create life together.*

Romance—How to Find It and Keep It from **Meditations for Deepening Love © 1994, 2010**

Now, the question for men is, do you see into the soul of woman? Do you see her unity? Eternal love cannot be yours until you do. When you do, eternal love cannot be denied you. And women, do you see the soul of man, his individuality? Do you see that man holding the division of male and female with all his might just for you? That is where your eternal love lies. To enter the sanctuary of love we must know that very soul of our sexual other. And I will tell you that the distinct essences of male and female will never change. Male and female are from the beginning and will always be. Together they form what we call family. From their love come children. And life goes on. Love is, in its essence, procreative. Everything a male and female do together is creative. Everything they do together is created out of their love. Male and female are in eternal love together right now! Their love is happening right now. Each of us is actually in eternal love with our sexual other half right now. When you know it so will you see it.

Mind and Spirit from **Selected Writings—Volume 2 © 1991, 2010**

Let us end this section by taking a moment to actually commune with that sexual opposite or other half of ourselves. Let's go within ourselves to the deep recesses of our hearts and feel the essence of that other. Let's for at least one moment close the fissure of unconsciousness between our souls and release the heartbreak and pain held within our beings. Let us heal ourselves in the balance of man and woman.

Man, commune with woman. Feel that woman in your life. Whether you be single or married, young or old, feel your connection with woman, your woman. Send her your love as male, wherever she may be in this universe. Tell her you are the one who will care for her, that you are ready to lay down your life for her as no one else. Let her know that you will do whatever it takes to secure her soul and implant new life into her being.

And woman, you, too, talk to man. Let your man know of your love, that you are there for him ready to take him into your being. Let him know that you, female, are the only one for him. Guide him to you. Commune to him your presence so he may find you. Whisper to him through his dreams so he can come only to you in his life quest, driving his male force into you so you may continue to bring forth life anew, a sexual life, male or female, in body, mind, and spirit.

The Spirit of Truth or of God © 2015

We, *man and woman,* ask for answered prayer. We ask in the name of the *Father* and the *Mother* of which there can be no separation. We ask that our love giveth *birth-life-death-rebirth*...to all things. We ask that what is given to us, we may give in return. We ask that the *spirit of truth* be the *spirit of love.* We ask that *God* be *life* and that *life* never be separate from our *interconnection* together. We pray for the *birth* of our children and the *rebirth* of our parents—that we may hold each in the same graces. We pray that this *procreant* spirit within us guide us—and never allow us to seek the "higher authority" over each other or anyone else. We ask that those most hurt amongst us never again be separated from *our* love or we separated from *their* love. *Thank you Father and Mother for hearing our prayer as your own and answering in your perfect timing as our own.*

Let the Light Shine Through from **Meditations for Deepening Love © 1994, 2010**

The still center is that point of perfect (man and woman) balance or stillness, also called the light, where knowing and fulfillment come together. It is the source-point of co-creation where we, out of our stillness, may "define it," "have it," and "let it go." If we could just hold to the stillness within ourselves—the balance with another—our experience would be one of always having it, and we would, for in the stillness we are one with our desire. We would have it and then could give it away, to watch it return as we again define it. Whatever it is we desire in life, only as we give it out of ourselves do we then receive it unto ourselves.

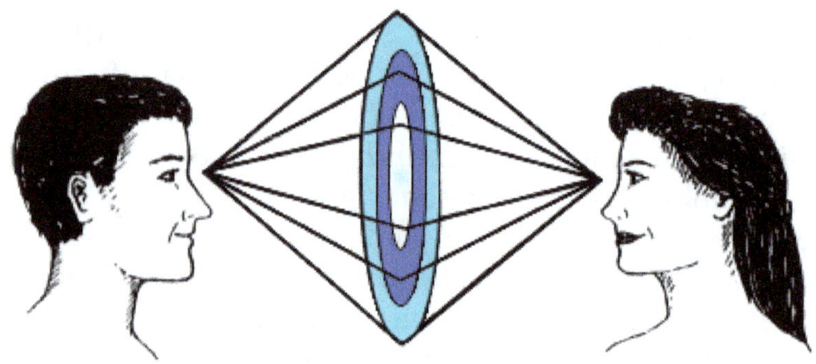

The Metaphysics of Sex...in a Changing World! © 2014

...there is not one moment in this universe, seen or unseen, where a man is not linked to a woman and a woman is not linked to a man.

The Man and Woman Spiritual Center from **Meditations for Deepening Love © 1994, 2010**

The Man and Woman Spiritual Center is only expressed in an actual touch between a man and a woman. It cannot be expressed in any other way. That touch may range from a momentary conscious recognition to a full embrace, but a touch, one to another, it is. The Spiritual Center is not expressed through belief, pledge, worship, ritual, or the paying of alms. It is not something that can be institutionalized, dogmatized, or ratified. There isn't any prescribed path to take, master to follow, or status to attain for its expression. There is only a man and a woman, touching and expressing creation together.

The Divine Touch: A New Creation For Life © 2021

The time has now come. The Divine Touch enters into us now.

To be touched by the Divine Touch is now of our time for, as we all know, there is no other time but now.

We cannot wait any longer for this touch. Waiting is only proof that we know it not.

We cannot pray for this touch. Prayer is only proof that we know it not.

We cannot believe in or worship this touch. Belief and worship are only proofs that we know it not.

We cannot ask our religious, educational, or political leaders to provide for us this touch. Asking them certainly is proof that we know it not.

Only an actual touch will do and the actual touch is the Divine Touch.

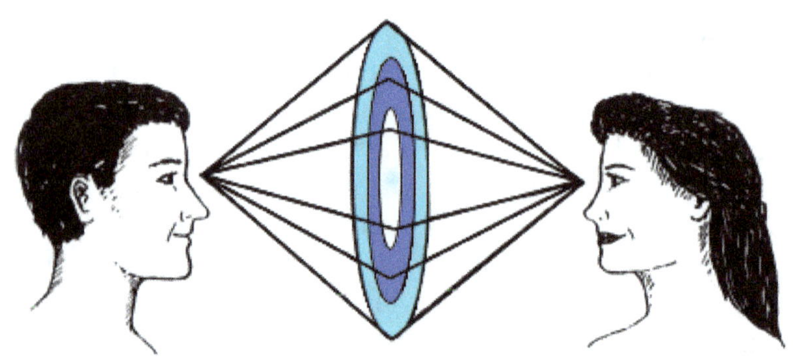

The message of Man and Woman Balance is simply about a TOUCH, one unto another. The TOUCH is the BALANCE is the PROCREANT! This spiritual touch transcends time. It also transcends death. I have often said that some of my best friends are "dead" philosophers. I speak with them and they speak with me. Not so much in words but rather in that of a deep feeling, a connection of heart/spirit. I speak with Mom and Dad; with Walter and Lao Russell. I speak with Jesus and with Cassandra (the Holy Spirit of Woman). I speak with Robert and Ron. I speak to Kahlil Gibran and Walt Whitman. One time during the IRS years, I was delivering some paperwork to the judge overseeing the case at the Federal Building in San Francisco. I had parked my car and was walking to the Federal Building. Many people were walking by. Suddenly, I began to see everyone as "God." "There goes God with a limp." "There goes God chatting with another." "There goes God suffering so".... I took a right around the corner and suddenly I saw the face of Walt Whitman, big, bright, and smiling at me. And I instantly knew that the experience I just had was what he had had as well. This is the TOUCH. You can call it ETERNAL LIFE. I call it SPIRITUAL PROCREATION. LET THERE BE LIFE!

To Cassandra—Early Years © 1985, 1994

The Light

It has been said
That buried deep within the heart
Beneath all "the truths"
There lies a stillness
That is the light
A light so bright
That we cannot see.
For so long
This light has been shining
---For no one to see?---
For so long ... the day came
When the light, broken-hearted
Began to weep
And its brightness
Turned to beauty.
And the light looked upward
Towards the night and said
"I am broken,"
And in that moment
Suddenly, everyone could see
This dimming light
And they laughed, saying to it
"You are not so bright."

The light recoiled
Pulling itself inward
To protect its wound
And buried itself
Beneath all "the truths"...
A light so bright ...

Request for Help

Marc and Mark,

I am writing this is to ask for your help. I'm tired. My 3 year stay at the various homeless shelters and current 3+ year stay at the Senior's Assisted Living complex has taken a toll.* But during that time, I did not resign myself to fate. I pressed on. I was able to complete six writings. The publishing part for five of those writings still remains.

*I remember, Marc, when I came to visit you in August of 2019. You had scheduled a session for me with your Teacher. I asked the question, "What is up with this financial collapse and homelessness? She responded, "This is the fastest way for you to go to get to where you want to be!" I draw on that most every day.

And you Mark, the Letter of Recommendation you wrote for me; it was so important in my being approved for the Senior Assisted Living complex. A life saver for sure.

Below is a list of writings I have completed during these past 6+ years. *Reflections on Light From A Homeless Shelter* has been published. *The Divine Touch: A New Creation for Life!* has been sent to First Edition Design Publishing and I have covered that cost. (First Edition Design Publishing has published all my writings to date and they have an extensive global reach. Moreover, I just got word that they will begin to put all my previous books "back up into their system at no charge and all annual fees will be waived." Very nice of them!) The remaining writings have all been copyrighted but not yet published. I have received estimates from First Edition Design Publishing for the publication of the remaining writings. They do both e-books and Print on Demand Softcover and Hardcover. Prices vary as to what one orders, just an e-book all the way to hardcover in color. My order is for e-book and Softcover book in color plus book cover/art for each book. Cost is $599 for e-book and Softcover book plus $150 for book cover/art. Total per book is $749. The last two books are smaller, more like pamphlets, and I am not sure of their cost. I have a request into them to clarify the cost of the pamphlets.I I am asking for financial help so I may finish the job—some 45 years of writing. Please let me know if you can help out with *Meditation as Spiritual Procreation* or *Selected Writings–Volume 3: A New Trinity.* Doesn't have to be for the whole amount; times are hard. Anything will help, gift or loan, $50, $100, $200, $400... today or in a month of two. It will take me some time to review each writing as it is sent to me. Whether you want to assist or not please feel free to send this e-mail on to family or friends who you think might have an interest.

Reflections on Light: From a Homeless Shelter © 2021, 170 pages, published.

The Divine Touch: A New Creation for Life! © 2021, 263 pages. Sent in to FEDP, cost covered.

Meditation as Spiritual Procreation © 2023, 353 pages. $749.

Selected Writings – Volume 3: A New Trinity © 2024, 393 pages. $749.

The Man and Woman Balance Invitation Package © 2023, 59 pages. (Not sure of cost as this is more of a pamphlet.)

Humanitarian Project: Man and Woman Balance © 2023, 71 pages. (Not sure of cost as this is more of a pamphlet.)

Selected Writings – Volume 3: A New Trinity is my last and final writing.* Brings me full circle if you will, right back to the Russell's *The Divine Trinity,* right back to the four of us who were a part of this journey. I am also in the process of bringing back-up the website of my writings. That will take another 2 – 3 months and will probably be an ongoing cost. Currently that is costing $120/month.

*Perhaps this small treatise would make a lasting final writing!

Please give thought to this. We go back a long way. You two are my spiritual brothers. I believe we have a connection to life, as I have with Robert, and with Ron, and with sweet Giselle who I go on a walkie with most every day and who has encouraged me throughout this writing, and David Leal who helped me navigate through the shelter years. And let me not forget Chris and Vera Zeek from High School. They have helped me as well.

I love you both,

Chris

The Man and Woman Balance
Invitation Package

Christopher Alan Anderson © 2023

www.manandwomanbalance.com

Contents

An Invitation

You are being invited to join in the movement called Man and Woman Balance. Man and Woman Balance is the name given to the Procreant Process of Life. Its premise is that Man and Woman are the two necessary parts of a continuum called the Lineage of Life. This Lineage of Life is an eternal process. It is comprised of two primary forces, a male force and a female force. Together these two sexual forces interact, upon which the Lineage of Life constitutes itself and continues onward. It is a Living Process, Birth-Life-Death-Rebirth....

This conception of Man and Woman Balance came to me in my early twenties, undoubtedly through my study of the writings of Walter and Lao Russell at the University of Science and Philosophy. It is a metaphysical/spiritual shift, not an experience of "physical sex/free love" like what came out of the sixties.

In my late twenties, 1979 or there about, I had an experience in that I saw a light and heard the words, "Your purpose is to bring the Message of Man and Woman Balance to the World!" Well, here we are, 2023, and that is still my purpose. I just now know I cannot do this by myself alone.

The enclosed materials are for those who want to better understand this Primacy of Life called **Man and Woman Balance**. It is intended to give to you an outline of its essence as the Primary Given of Life. Moreover, it provides a new way forward out of what seems like an insurmountable crevasse that only seems to being heartache to our hearts and souls. Take a look around you, chaos and collapse all around us. Pick your field, religion, sexuality, psychology, economics and politics, science, etc.; they lack a center. Our Center-point, or what we thought it was or believed it to be, cannot hold. Could it be that, fundamentally, this is due to the fact that we have yet to fully understand the Process of Creation itself?

It has been my objective for some 44 now years to create this new way forward. Why? Because, to date, we have not based our fundamental conceptual understanding, not to mention our Soul Essence, on the Life Process itself. This may have greater clarity when you read the passage under the title **"Foundation of Man and Woman Balance website © 2012:"**

Let me mention that the whole basis and understanding of Man and Woman Balance lies in its definition. The term balance, as I am using it, means Equal and Opposite. Is this to suggest that You and I, at some level, exist in such a relationship? YES. At a most fundamental level of existence.

What follows are samples from my writings, my hope being that from these samples you can capture the breath and scope of this paradigm shift that I offer. Why do I offer it? Because I cannot do it alone. As you read through the materials, see if something doesn't touch your heart and soul, if only for a moment. One touch; that is all it takes to make this shift. Much work needs to be done, and everyone is invited and has a place. Let us begin...*

*Some of the selections are from earlier writings and the context or example they are referenced in may be dated.

Author's Bio

I was brought up in a Christian home with loving parents and three older brothers. In high school, I found myself becoming interested in literature. In my twenties that interest turned to philosophy, mainly metaphysics. I was struggling with a question—how did it go—is ultimate reality a one or a many? I rephrased that to say—a one or a two. Somehow it occurred to me that ultimate reality is both a one and a two. We hear in the good book that the two unite as one. (Matthew 19:4-6). But how about the one dividing into two; isn't that of equal necessity? I came up with a saying, *"One is not without the other; both are needed for either to be."* Like breathing; how could breathing occur without both inhalation and exhalation? Or the sexes; how could life work without both male and female? This was my thinking at the time.

During this time, in my twenties, thoughts would come to my mind. I began writing. I wrote into my thirties. Much of it I didn't fully understand at the time. I published my first writing, *The Man and Woman Relationship: A New Center for the Universe,* in 1985. And yes, I had to self-publish; who was there to understand this?

Today I have written some twenty plus books and many articles and booklets. They are all on this same theme, that the center of things is an and. Moreover, that this and exists in a frame of equal and opposite, i.e., *sexual*. And think about it, how could there be life and all its progression without a dual creative process—what I call procreation or in metaphysical terms spiritual procreation? As I state on the www.manandwomanbalance.com website: "Mankind has yet to distinguish the two sexes on the spiritual level. In this failure lies the root of our problems and why we cannot yet touch the eternal together. The message of man and woman balance brings each of us together in love with our eternal other half right now." I also state: "Love is the only state of existence between male and female.—Male and female are in love together, forever." Awesome!

I have now come to understand that the purpose of these writings, my life purpose, is to unite the spiritual and the procreative as one. How could we consider them not?

Christopher Alan Anderson

Man and Woman Balance Website © 2012:

On a personal note, when Mr. Anderson was asked to describe the writings and what he felt their message was he responded, "Spiritual procreation. Mankind has yet to distinguish the two sexes on the spiritual level. In this failure lies the root of our problems and why we cannot yet touch the eternal together. The message of Man and Woman Balance brings each of us together in love with our eternal other half right now."

Mission Statement

"Bringing Man and Woman Together!"

...constitutes a shift into the new paradigm of a two-force universe of spiritual procreation.

The Man and Woman Manifesto: What We Believe!
Christopher Alan Anderson © 2017

In *The Man and Woman Manifesto: What We Believe!*, the author gives an accounting of what this paradigm shift into Man and Woman Balance is about, both individually and for the world at large. We are at a turning point in the conscious evolution of mankind on planet earth. We all feel the change, and turbulence, although we are not sure of which way to turn. We are being offered an empty sexual progressivism through L,G,B,T,Q, as well as an existential threat in Islamic radicalism. In the meantime, our own Constitutional system of governance with its Christian roots seems to comprise a history—what is the way forward? These are not easy questions. This is not an easy book. But if you can capture its essence your life will forevermore have purpose. This writing will forevermore change your life as well as the world at large.

Comments from Facebook
July 11, 2017

Dawn M. Dawset (UK): A well over due awakening. My conceptual consciousness has often naturally thought upon these lines of teachings, a huge subject of truth to me. I'm inspired by your work. It's definitely a ground breaking read. Thank you.

Writings by Christopher Alan Anderson

The Discovery of Life © 1994

For aeons, mankind has been caught in a trap, a trap so hideous it has prevented men and women from achieving any type of enduring success. Yet, from this trap our religions formed and promised mankind a way out through another world. Later, our socio-political institutions were formed, promising us liberation in this world. Yet, neither could deliver, for they were part of the trap, which was nothing but a simple misconception mankind made at the dawn of consciousness preventing him from discovering life.

This writing is about understanding and correcting that misconception whereupon mankind, for the first time, may discover life, thereby bringing a fulfillment and completion to his (or her) self.

The Man and Woman Relationship: A New Center for the Universe © 1985, 2010

The answer to this "mystery" of unity lies in the fact that there isn't any unity in and of itself alone. This is the great misunderstanding of the ages. Unity is only one part or parameter point, just as is individuality, in a two-way sequential process. The mistake the spiritualists make is in thinking of unity as the whole, sole, or real reality. The materialists also make that mistake, equating the material world of dimension/form as the sole reality. But equally so, we cannot know of a sole individuality without its relation to unity.

Unity then is known only as a context point in relation to individuality. It may be said that unity in its context to individuality is different than individuality and thus we can capture its sense in that relationship. We do—at each moment of its existence.

The Two Forces of Creation, 1988—Selected Writings, Volume 2 © 1991, 2010

In review, let me suggest that "what is" is relationship-in-process. Relationship-in-process is fundamental or primordial, not a First Cause or One Force. This is to further say that there isn't a supreme being although there may be supreme beings. There isn't a mover of the spheres although there may be movers of the spheres. There isn't a one God who sees all that becomes or forms all immortal beings although there may be gods that do just that.* There is not a single fundamental primordial creative force in the universe, i.e. energy, desire, motive, impulse, purpose, impetus, drive, intention, nature, will, consciousness. Prana, mana, Ki. Chi, Waken, bioplasma, light, cosmic energy, life force, vital pulse, or Holy Spirit. There is only one force in relationship to another force from which creation may then occur. We have to date made a critical mistake in not noting this elementary fact within our conception of order.

*Some language from the early Greek philosopher Pythagoras, 570-500 B.C.

The Discovery of Life © 1994

The metaphysical center of creation is a dividing/uniting sexual creative process between the two forces of male and female in perfect balance together. It is this creative dynamic of man and woman balance that will replace the old static one-force conception, for man and woman balance has always been and will always be. There isn't any other process, principle, or order in the universe that will bring forth life for it is life.

...and the TWO shall become as ONE—Encoded in the Book of Eternal Life © 2010; Meditations for Deepening Love © 2010

In the heart of every man and woman, the TWO, is placed the eternal desire to become as ONE. This desire is known as love. "May I give my life to you," the man shouts. "Yes, please do," the woman responds. And out of this love a new birth of life, a new born boy or girl, is brought forth as the eternal desire moves on. The ONE has just become the TWO again. This eternal process is called the *procreant*—a procreative process of balanced interchange between the TWO and the ONE.

And so the TWO becomes as ONE. Not a ONE of no TWO, but a TWO within a ONE for, procreantly, every ONE will again become a TWO. Within the ONE is always the divided TWO. Within the TWO is always the united ONE. And so the 'AS ONE' is actually a BALANCE between the dividing TWO and the uniting ONE. This balance is sexual in that the parts dividing and uniting are opposite pairs, opposite meaning sexual as in male and female pairs. *Sexual balanced interchange* is this procreant and eternal process, the ONE dividing into sexual opposites (the TWO) and the TWO uniting into the sexual equilibrium or rest of the ONE.

Love: The Law of Polar Opposites—The 2008-2009 Articles © 2010

Only (sexual) opposites can unite to again divide...creating the spiritual lineage of (procreant) love.

I Carry the Cross, too—The Completion of the Message of Jesus Christ © 1992; Man, Woman, and God © 1994, 2010

What I am speaking of here is a spirituality, one that is connected to creation itself. It is important that we understand that the door to the spiritual light is through the creative embrace. We just cannot consciously connect in spirit without knowing the surrender of life to our other half. We are still living in a time where there is a gap between spirituality and sexuality. Thus, we have proceeded to taint sexuality with sin and guilt, or else cheapen it with promiscuity. From this imbalance, we, men and women, have not held ourselves in a pure heart. The pure heart is the clean heart. It knows not the trace of sin (imbalance). The pure heart sees "God" at every moment. When a man looks into a woman and sees her soul (unity), so he sees God. When a woman looks into a man and sees his soul (individuality), she, too, sees God. God is only revealed as we, man and woman, look into each other and see each other's soul.

Aristotle Laws Revised and Sexed

<u>Identity</u>—Male is Male; Female is Female.

<u>Non-Contradiction</u>—Male is not Female; Female is not Male.

<u>Excluded Middle</u>—What is not Male is Female; what is not Female is Male. (Everything is either Male or Female.)

<u>Interconnection</u>*—Male is interconnected to Female; Female is interconnected to Male. (One is not without the other; both are needed for either to be.)

*The Law of Interconnection was originally called the Law of Connection by Hungarian philosopher Akos Pauler (1876-1933). I am calling it Interconnection and adding the statement 'One is not without the other; both are needed for either to be.'

Dimensions in Consciousness © 1990; Selected Writings: Volume 2 © 1991, 2010

Who am 'I'?

'I' am a male in relationship to a female,
or
'I' am a female in relationship to a male,
. . . whichever sexuality 'I' happen to be,
'You' being the sexual opposite of me.

Why am 'I' here?

'I' am here to express the sexuality that 'I' am . . .

Male, being that force which seeks to individualize a form separate and apart from the unity of male-female.

Female, being that force which seeks to unite separate forms together from the division of male and female.

. . . so that together we may continue to manifest our own sexual creation.

The Man and Woman Relationship

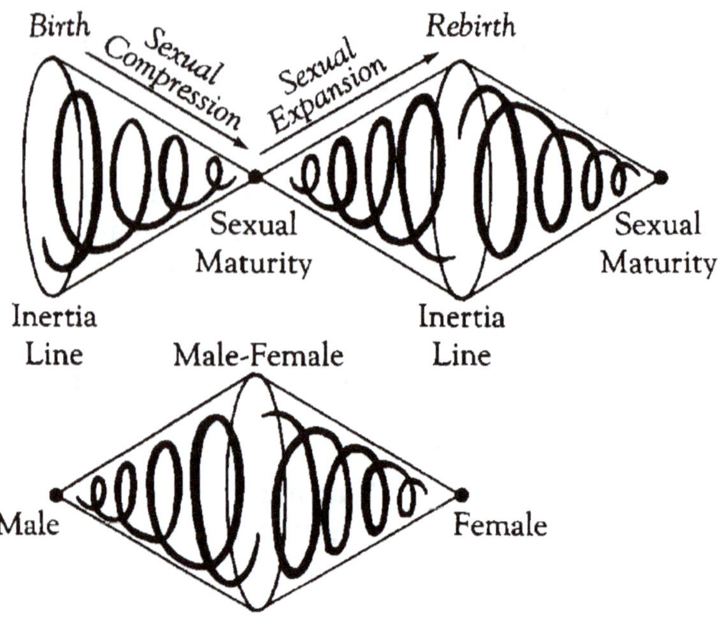

The Universal Religion: The Final Destiny of Mankind © 1994

A child is born represents the touch of love (balance) between a man and a woman. That one touch is the whole foundation of the universe. It is a direct touch, a complete touch. It is the touch of life. All that is required for this touch is a man and a woman, conscious of their creativity (connection) together. In their consciousness of life, they touch and—a child is born. This touch is the truth of life. There isn't any greater truth than life. In the universal religion, only the two forces exist expressing their love and their life. There isn't anything else but a male and a female in creative balance. Nothing else is recognized for nothing else exists. This perfect state of creative balance is known as God. Why? Because from this balance a child can be born.

The Eternal Marriage © 1992; Man, Woman, and God © 1994, 2010

The spiritual connection is a connection between a man and a woman whereby they recognize their eternal creation and love together. It is based in their sexual differentiation from and creative need for each other. In this, a man and woman have life purpose together. They are the co-creators of all that is. The formed universe moves through them. They together hold the balance on which all life depends. The world moves one step forward into the light with just one touch of their love.

Meditations for Deepening Love © 1995, 2010

Meditation to Son from Father

My dear Son, you were only just a babe, and now look at you. You have come through the years well; you've grown into your own manhood ready to take on the responsibilities thereof. What more could I ask for? What would make me happier than to see you now in your place in life, securing your life and family? I remember the many esoteric talks we have had over the years while you were struggling over the great questions, seeking to discover the meaning of life. But now they are answered for you, aren't they? Your actions tell me so as you have found the priority of your family. And so I tried to tell you, my son, in my actions. Do you now know why my family always came first with me? But now I am growing old. Things are in your hands now. You lead the world, in your own way. You take your place amongst the great, in your own way. You keep your family together, and through your actions teach your son the meaning of life. And in that thought I will go to my rest, always knowing, always proud, that you are my son.

Meditation to Daughter from Mother

My dearest daughter, how could I have ever told you what it means to be a woman? Yes, you thought you knew; at times you were so sure, you would look at me wondering what I knew about life. But now you know, don't you? Yes, my blessed daughter, you, too, have now crossed the channel from woman to mother. You, too, have given birth to a baby, your baby. And now you know; I could see it in your eyes when you first held your baby to your breast. You, my daughter, have brought forth life, just as I had done. And then the look you gave me showing me your understanding, and love, that I am your mother and you are my child, just as you are now the mother of your child. Now you know, my daughter, why I could not explain motherhood in its purpose in my life to you, just as you won't be able to explain it to your daughter. She, too, must first give birth to know herself and her mother. Thank you, my daughter, for now knowing me as your mother and knowing yourself as my daughter.

The Man and Woman Manifesto: Let the Revolution Begin © 1994

Family is the sovereign unit of all creation. It stands at the hub or center of life. It is the source of all things. A family is, by definition, composed of a male and a female. The two equal but opposite forces are in play, dividing and uniting together. From each unity of a male and a female comes procreation, a reproduction of life. Family is the most essential thing in all of life. It is life.

Man, Woman, and God © 1994, 2010

Men, do you know that the soul of woman has been hurt? You have hurt your woman, haven't you? You left her behind to bleed on the roadside. You used and discarded her when all she wanted was to love you. Why do you do this? Do you not see that woman is the only bridge that will take you beyond yourself? Woman is your only hope, but due to your actions she is giving up her belief in you. Can you, man, take responsibility for creating this state of affairs? Can you feel every pain that you have ever caused woman, from her birth to her death?

Women, do you know the spirit of man has been hurt? You blame man for all the havoc around you, don't you? You think that men "just don't get it" and that you could do a better job at life. Can you? In the name of equality, you kill the spirit of life, the difference that you and men depend upon. Now, you only want a man conditionally, not completely. Cannot you see that without a man you can't even have yourself? Perhaps men, too, are doing the best they know how and that in their hearts they only want to care for you. Will you allow that? Can you feel a man's very struggle throughout all of time to do only one thing, to make a home for you? Can you feel this when you are alone?

Dimensions in Consciousness © 1990; Selected Writings: Volume 2 © 1991, 2010

Love is not separated from the metaphysic one holds concerning the nature of reality. If that metaphysic is creatively imbalanced, what then does that say about the availability of love? Love springs forth out of creative balance. It is the act of creation itself.

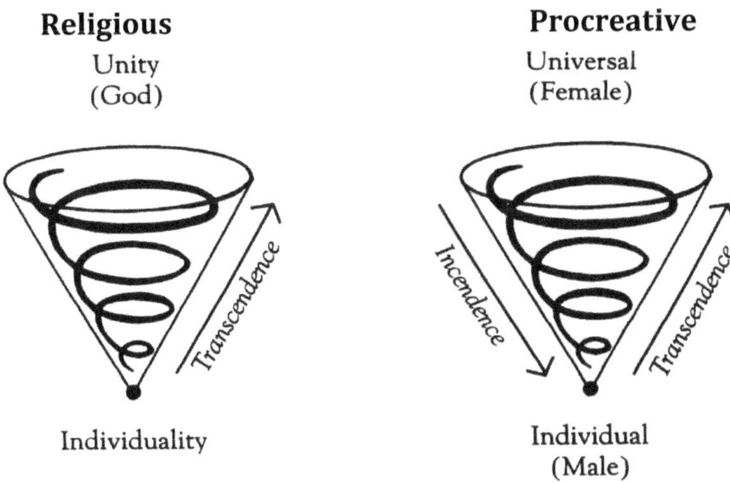

I Carry the Cross, too—The Completion of the Message of Jesus Christ © 1992; Man, Woman, and God © 1994, 2010

Sexual metaphysics is the comparative study of any given, i.e., conception, paradigm, or model to see if it meets the test of procreation and thereby holds to the one universal standard or law of creative balance. The fact that there is an absolute reality (creative balance) gives us the metaphysic of life that we must be aligned to if we intend to sustain life.

Man and Woman Balance—Equal and Opposite
Masculinism—Opposite but not Equal
Feminism—Equal but not Opposite

Structural Balance

Man and Woman Balance

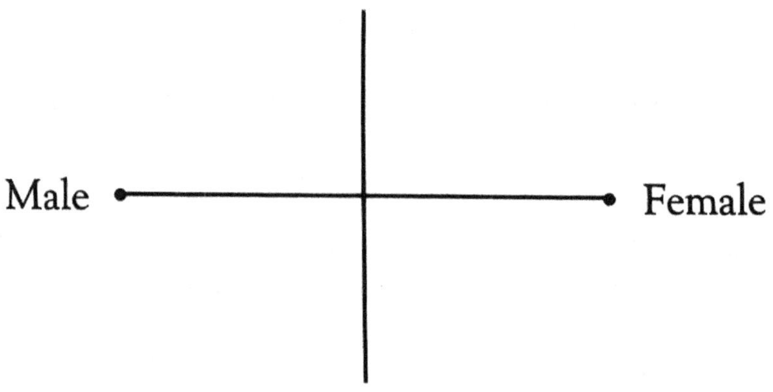

Structural Imbalance

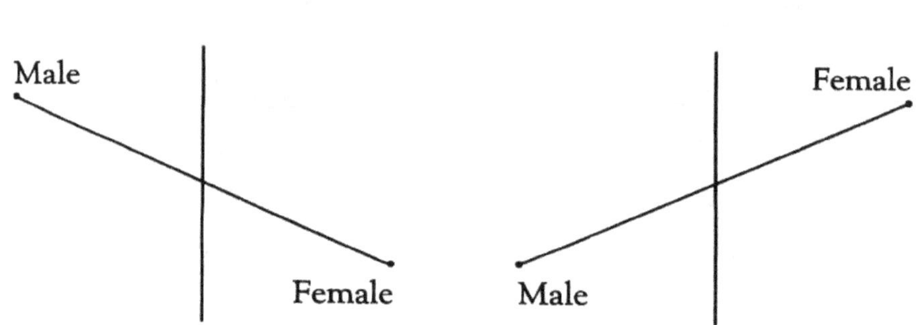

Homosexuality is not a Sexuality—The 2008-2009 Articles © 2010

Neither Masculinism nor Feminism, in any of its forms, can bring us to a true union (fullness) where the two become as one. Union of opposites is a metaphysic issue concerning the order/nature of the universe itself. Call that order a dual or a primary or a two forces or a 1st pair—it is the primordial male and female. Our purpose as man and woman pairs is to touch in love and in so doing create life together.

The Spiritual Components in the Lives of Men and Women—The 2008-2009 Articles © 2010

Masculinism is an unequal polarization between man and woman. Feminism is an equal depolarization between man and woman. Man and woman balance is an equal polarization between man and woman. Today, at least in the West, we see this great shift from masculinism to feminism sweeping over everything as if feminism somehow is the answer. Just as the spiritual components of life could not be found in masculinism, nor will they be able to be found in feminism. Only in the balance can a man and a woman reach out to each other in that one moment of their procreant love. They, man and woman, (pro)creating each moment together, are the only standard.

Spiritual Procreation: Faith is the Substance—The 2008-2009 Articles © 2010

Both masculinism and feminism preclude us from entering into the *faith* that is *the substance of things hoped for, the evidence of things not seen.* Neither one of them can take us to a new metaphysical channel that we can now call *faith as procreant substance.* Only *spiritual procreation,* i.e., *procreant love,* i.e., *man and woman balance* can do that. Our faith is answered in the tangible, the real, the concrete substance of *spiritual procreation.* It is from *spiritual procreation* that we see the evidence. And what do we see? We see the *procreant love* we have with our *eternal other half* as it exists in our hearts right now, reflected out into the world as the world at each and every moment. A new day has dawned.

Our Purpose Together—Bringing the Eternal Down to Earth—The 2008-2009 Articles © 2010

Neither masculinism nor feminism, in any of its forms, can bring the eternal down to earth. This is now for us (man and woman pairs) to do. It is our purpose to touch in love together and, by doing so, we, man and woman, bring the eternal down to earth. We do this by living our love in our lives. The eternal is always a procreant balance between metaphysical primaries or duals. There isn't anything more sacred, in the light, or of eternal life than that one procreant touch between one man and one woman right now. That one touch will last forever when you know it.

Meditation As Spiritual Procreation © 2023

This Frame of Sexual Balance defines for us a **New Trinity**. The Russell's called this frame **The Divine Trinity**. We may also call it **The Holy Trinity**. From a philosophical perspective we can just call it the **Frame of Sexual Balance** or **Man and Woman Balance.** Its defining characteristics are <u>Equal and Opposite</u>. It thereby discloses the Frame of Sexual <u>Im</u>balance as being either Masculinism (Opposite but not Equal) or Feminism (Equal but not Opposite). Now imagine, for example, you are in meditation not knowing the frame from which you are attached to and embedded in. Is it Masculinism? Perhaps it is Feminism. The same can be said of prayer. How many of us pray from an imbalanced core within ourselves? I mean, would not that make a difference? Perhaps a HUGE difference. Historically our frame has been mostly Masculinism (Opposite but not Equal). After all, wasn't woman made for man, made from man's rib? Lately, the Feminist frame of Equal but not Opposite has taken hold. Are you WOKE?

Meditation As Spiritual Procreation © 2023

We have been caught in a trap. Today it might be called a Matrix! It is the Black Hole of the Abyss. It is called <u>Man and Woman Imbalance</u> which shows itself as Masculinism (Opposite but not Equal) or Feminism (Equal but not Opposite). Let's look at another diagram. What does this tell you?

Sexual Metaphysics

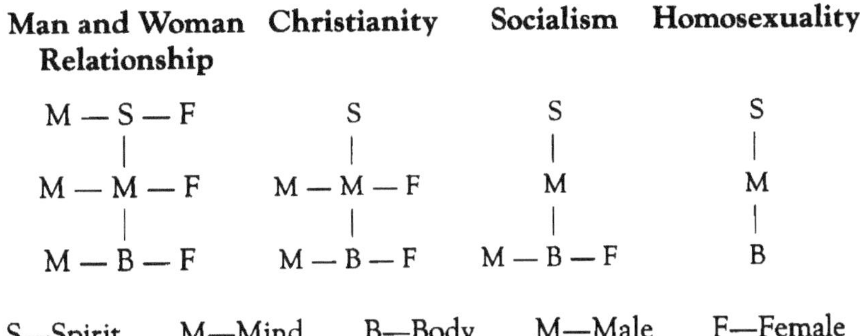

S—Spirit M—Mind B—Body M—Male F—Female

First, we see the Frame of Man and Woman Balance (Equal and Opposite). Notice that this frame sexes (Equal and Opposite) the Spiritual, Mental, and Physical realms. Then we move to Christianity. This frame only sexes the Mental and Physical realms. It leaves the Spiritual realm unsexed. Then we move to Socialism. Here we see only one realm holding the sexual distinction, the Physical; the two other realms are unsexed. And lastly, we move to Homosexuality with all realms unsexed. Man and Woman Balance, Christianity, Socialism, and Homosexuality were the names I used back when this understanding first came to me sometime around 1990–1991. I called this understanding (or study) **Sexual Metaphysics**. We could also use the names Sexual Balance, Creationalism, Humanism, and Homosexuality or, perhaps today, Man and Woman Balance, Religion, Politics, and LGBTQ.

Romance—How to Find it and Keep it © 1991; Meditations for Deepening Love © 1995, 2010

Now, the question for men is, do you see into the soul of woman? Do you see her unity? Eternal love cannot be yours until you do. When you do, eternal love cannot be denied you. And women, do you see the soul of man, his individuality? Do you see that man holding the division of male and female with all his might just for you? That is where your eternal love lies. To enter the sanctuary of love we must know that very soul of our sexual other. And I will tell you that the distinct essences of male and female will never change. Male and female are from the beginning and will always be. Together they form what we call family. From their love come children. And life goes on. Love is, in its essence, procreative. Everything a male and female do together is creative. Everything they do together is created out of their love. Male and female are in eternal love together right now! Their love is happening right now. Each of us is actually in eternal love with our sexual other half right now. When you know it so will you see it.

The Man and Woman Spiritual Center © 1990; Illumination © 1990, 2010

The Man and Woman Spiritual Center is only expressed in an actual touch between a man and a woman. It cannot be expressed in any other way. That touch may range from a momentary conscious recognition to a full embrace, but a touch, one to another, it is. The Spiritual Center is not expressed through belief, pledge, worship, ritual, or the paying of alms. It is not something that can be institutionalized, dogmatized, or ratified. There isn't any prescribed path to take, master to follow, or status to attain for its expression. There is only a man and a woman, touching and expressing creation together.

To Cassandra—Early Years © 1985, 1994

Serenity

Cassandra
Do you know
How much I could love you
Even through your change
From a woman in need
To a mother with seed
Passing your desire onward
And loyalty too.
How much I could love you
Even through my change
From a man of deed
To a father losing his lead
Becoming second to your child
Just as it should be.

Christ Jesus Channeled—An Open Letter to Mankind © 1988; Meditations for Deepening Love © 1995, 2010

...As I stand before you I now say that I, the Christ, am nothing of myself alone. *I AM* only as I am with woman. I create only as I create with woman. I love only as I love woman. I know truth only as I know woman. I speak only as I listen to woman. It is woman who now speaks through me...

My Christ-child, have you finally cometh for me. As long as you have been waiting to truly express your love, I have been waiting to receive it unto me. I can no longer be content to receive only a part of you. I desire all of you. Do you know that it is I, woman, who receives your being and rests your very soul? Do you realize that your rebirth is only through me, that I reproduce all that you create? My Christ-man, I don't seek to take your place; I only want to be by your side. I have only wanted to know that above all else, I, woman, am yours, that your concern for me is without boundary. Take all of me and never let me go for I, too, am ready for you. It is our time. This time you will have woman. This time you will have me. Let us walk arm and arm into the creation that is ours together.

My friends, do you hear these words of woman channeled through me? You see, only woman can complete my message. I alone have nothing to say. The Christ saga is finished. I have come again to be with a woman, to marry her and have children with her. What would you have me do? For two thousand years now I have been holding you. That is how long my crucifixion has been. Let me now release into woman and *live.* Why should that upset you so? Or will you insist on holding a belief in me? But you now must know, creation is only through male and female. All of the illuminants down through the ages haves missed this truth. The universe is of male and female creation through which we are born, and live, die, and are reborn.... There is nothing else.

Please know my friends, my heart is too heavy but to speak this truth. I, too, have been through much. I can only stand before you as your equal. I don't demand from you your acceptance of my words. In many ways, I am what is in the way of man and woman fully uniting together in spirit. I would only hope with all of my being that you, man, love your woman with all your heart, and you, woman, love your man with all your heart. That is all there ever really was to say. And now we both can know *the peace that passeth all understanding.*

My time has now come. I will be leaving you. I will not return. You know where I will be—*in every heart and home.* And so these words will be my last to you.

Anything that you desire to know. Anything that you need to know in existence, will only be revealed to you through your own other half, that sexual opposite of you. To know your other half along with yourself is to know all creation and your own immortality as creator with your other half.

This is my last truth. In light and love,

Christ Jesus

Mind and Spirit, © 1987; Selected Writings—Volume 2 © 1991, 2010

Let us end this section by taking a moment to actually commune with that sexual opposite or other half of ourselves. Let's go within ourselves to the deep recesses of our hearts and feel the essence of that other. Let's for at least one moment close the fissure of unconsciousness between our souls and release the heartbreak and pain held within our beings. Let us heal ourselves in the balance of man and woman.

Man, commune with woman. Feel that woman in your life. Whether you be single or married, young or old, feel your connection with woman, your woman. Send her your love as male, wherever she may be in this universe. Tell her you are the one who will care for her; that you are ready to lay down your life for her as no one else. Let her know that you will do whatever it takes to secure her soul and implant new life into her being.

And woman, you, too, talk to man. Let your man know of your love, that you are there for him ready to take him into your being. Let him know that you, female, are the only one for him. Guide him to you. Commune to him your presence so he may find you. Whisper to him through his dreams so he can come only to you in his life quest, driving his male force into you so you may continue to bring forth life anew, a sexual life, male or female, in body, mind, and spirit.

We Can Only Create Together

- Man and woman can only create together.
- From the love of a man and a woman new life, a son or a daughter, is born.
- All new born life is divine life.
- Each creation is a divine creation.
- Each creation is the most special creation.
- Each creation is bequeathed with the divine love of Father and Mother.
- Every creation has within its heart the desire to create life with and through its other half.

- Every creation is eternal in its procreative balance with its eternal other half.
- The heartbeat within every creation is the heartbeat of procreative love.
- Procreative love is the life-dynamic of the universe.
- Procreative love is God.
- God is Man and Woman Balance.
- God is expressed when a man and a woman reach out to each other and touch in the one pure, perfect moment of their most special love.
- Only together can a man and a woman create.

Healing In The Light © 1998

To All Men the World Over
To those of you who claim to know God, or some kind of human goodness...

Be it now known:

- **As you treat a woman, so do you treat God.**
- **As you honor a woman, so do you honor God.**
- **As you love a woman, so do you love God.**
- **As you hold tight to a woman, so do you hold tight to God.**
- **As you listen to a woman, so do you hear God.**
- **As you stand up for a woman, so do you stand up for God.**
- **As you walk with a woman, so do you walk with God.**
- **As you trust in a woman, so do you trust in God.**
- **As you cherish a woman, so do you cherish God.**

- **As you believe in a woman, so do you believe in God.**
- **As you have a child with a woman, so you have a child of God.**
- **As you hold to the very center of creation with a woman, so do you hold to the very center of creation with God.**
- **As you no longer look for God other than in a woman, so do you know the love of God.**

Let it now be known—your only avenue to God is in touching the very heart of a woman.

Wealth Plus+: Empowering Your Everyday!
© 2013

Declaration of Freedom

.Be it known, the following truths are self-evident...

We, the People of (   ), come to a turning point in our history, a time for each of us who seek a better life to recognize a simple yet immortal truth—*freedom.*

Freedom—That necessity required for an individual and/or people to create wealth. It is understood as a primary principle that wealth is generated from individual exertion not from government coercion.

Freedom—From which each man and woman have unalienable rights/intrinsic worth, not as a guarantee of our needs but as the opportunity of our lives—to pursue our own happiness, to make our way through our own efforts, and to receive the fruits of our own labor.

Freedom—The acknowledgment of our sovereignty, that we the people—both individually and collectively—stand as the sovereign and that government stands as our servant, never our master, and that the purpose of our government is to serve the common law—that order that arises around people's contracting through mutual consent.

Freedom—And lastly, let us understand that the test of freedom lies not in whether "I have mine," but rather in my own willingness to allow you to equally have your freedom. *"Can 'I' let others be free?"* Let that be our enduring question.

May the spirit of freedom forever touch each one of our souls.

Living in the Procreant (Holy) Spirit

Matthew 28:20: ...I am with you always, even unto the end of the world.

Today I awaken to the will of the Procreant (Holy) Spirit. "Ask me into your heart," she says. *Yes, woman, I hear these exact words.* She continues, "And please come into my heart and live in me." *I will.*

"Together, there isn't anything we can't do. But it must be together. Together we are One." She continues, "I so want to open my heart to you. For so long I have wanted to speak to you, man. Since the garden my true soul has been covered. Can you finally hear me now?" *Yes, I do hear you now.*

"Thank you. Thank you for listening to my very spirit as woman. I can only love you, a man. You give to me child. I can only love you with all my heart. I just want to express to you, no, give to you, my true heart. I want you to know what it means to me for you to give child to me." *Thank you. Thank you for receiving child from me. I don't always think of it that way.*

"Yes, I know. You want me." *I do.* "But whenever we come together so a child is spiritually seeded, even if it is just a small hello." *I understand that now.* "I need you so much. I give everything to you." *You do!* "So why do you hold back at times?" *Perhaps at times I need to be away from you. How else can I know how much I need you if I am not away from you?* "But you are not really away from me, are you?" *Not really. What I do I only do for you.*

"This love is our child. Our child is our love." *Our love is our child.* "Yes, you said it. That brings tears of joy to my eyes." *There can only be <u>our</u> love. And my <u>word</u> to you is: ...I am with you always, even unto the end of the world.*

Can you feel these words from the new construct of God the Father and God the Mother?; from God the Holy Son and God the Holy Daughter?; from God the living sexual spirit within you as male or as female—which ever sexuality you may be—always in connection with your equal and opposite other half? Within the Divine Trinity is the Divine Touch. Then you will walk the lands, hand-in-hand, as did Jesus and Mary Magdalene, shining the light of your sexual purity and rebirth for all to see. Then you will know that there cannot be male without female or female without male even if we are speaking of "God." Then you will know of your child abiding in the perfect balance of man

and woman. And then you will know that every day is resurrection day; the rebirth of life within our sexual souls.

The Divine Touch: A New Creation for Life © 2021

Channeling the Eternal Woman

Thank you. I am the *Eternal Woman*. I am not a "God." I am a woman. I am the female soul within every woman. As a woman, I stand with man. Actually, I stand between man and child. I am the link between man and child. I am the space between man and child. I am the death of all life and the life of all death. From a man dying inside of me, so our child is born out of me. I am what you might call the field, frame, zero-point, space, opening, womb, or void. But I am not death. Rather, I give life to death. I bring life-potential to all things. I connect all things within me. In this, I am love. Without me there would never be love. All women know this about me because they know it about themselves.

Channeling the Eternal Woman © 2014

The Lineage of Life!

...Be it known, the following truths are self-evident...

A man gives over his life essence to a woman. In this act a man is uniting his Soul with the Soul of a woman.

A woman receives that man into her life essence. The Two become as One. The woman gives back in birthing a new life essence through Son or Daughter. The One becomes as Two.

Through man a woman brings new life into sexual form, a Son or a Daughter. She also is giving back to man that he may give again.

This Sexual Process is the Soul of the Universe. It is not a singular process. A Two are required, an Equal and Opposite Two—Male and Female.

The Sexual Process is the center-point of Life. It is the Lineage of Life. Male and Female constitute the Lineage of Life. As such Male and Female must be considered to be the Primary of Life.

As a new birth is formed, Son or Daughter, and as that life grows, it seeks to find its own Equal and Opposite Sexual Other Half. Both Male and Female instinctively know as per their own Existence, that they don't exist of themselves alone. And so they seek that Sexual Other to complete themselves, as they know Creation/Lineage cannot exist by themselves alone.

"Seek and ye shall find, knock, and it shall be opened unto you...." and the door is opened, a man and a woman meet and know—the Two have already become as One. Husband and Wife they are in Spirit.

A man lays down his life so his wife may live again. A woman lays down her life so their Child may live again. A Child holds Father and Mother in his or her Soul as they, his or her Father and Mother, take their lasts breaths in this Life Incarnation. The Child has learned from his or her Father and Mother to walk the path as <u>Man</u> or <u>Woman</u>. The Child has learned the meaning of Commitment.

We, a Husband and a Wife, can only exist through Commitment. The whole of this Universe is held together, and given to birth new life, through a man and woman's Commitment to each other.

The Marriage Commitment, one Man and one Woman, holds the Secret to Eternal Life. Love ye one another—the Lineage of Life!

Website: www.manandwomanbalance.com

The Miracle

And so I ask, "Oh, dear God, why do you give me this much inner pain?" And God replies, "So the light will shine so brightly."

"And how must I pray?" I ask. God again replies, "You must pray to God the Father <u>and</u> God the Mother. To say this another way, you may pray from not just yourself alone but in the spirit of your togetherness with your equal and opposite sexual other half. Become a part of that perfect sexual procreant balance. Your light will so shine that it will touch another's soul and lift them up out of their own darkness. Believe, my Son, and so you shall receive."

"Thank you. But how may I receive the Miracle? I am not even sure I know what it is; my road has been so long."

"The Miracle, my Son, is the Resurrection. The Resurrection is simply the spiritual Rebirth of Life."

"And when does this take place?" I ask.

And God speaks his final words, "Right now."

The Divine Touch: A New Creation for Life © 2021

To Cassandra—Early Years © 1985, 1994

Transformation

Easing
Slightly
Almost without effort
And suddenly
I find myself
Drawn into you

Drawn into your being
Becoming a part
Of your very soul
From your beginning
On through to your ending
To a new beginning
Never to return out from you
As the same man.

The First Pair, © 2010; Meditations for Deepening Love, © 2010

The First Pair has come! We thought the return would be through Jesus or some Avatar type. It wasn't. We thought there would be a great rejoicing—some final salvation. There wasn't. We thought the return would bring peace on earth. It didn't. Certainly the return would at least better our plights. It didn't even do that. So what then was the return, what did it do? Perhaps—could it?—touch one heart.

Man: We, my beloved wife and I, have come forth to unite together that we may have child. If you understand what I have just said, you understand all things.

Woman: Our child, created out of our love—let that be the light that shines for us our way.

Man: If you don't understand what my wife and I just said, let me illuminate. We, the *First Pair*, are what you have, heretofore, called God. We are the first cause, the divine principle and purpose, the primal force(s), the source of all creation. All that is exists through us, our love.

Woman: The spirit of our love connects us all—from the first man and woman to the last which again becomes the first. It is this spirit that is the *Holy Spirit*. We, the *First Pair*, speak to you through our hearts.

Man: The first creation, our child, came from us out of the balance that we together comprise. Please understand, *balance* is the first principle. You cannot circumvent it. Balance always comprises an equal and opposite two—a man and a woman, *primordially*. That is its definition.

Woman: From our balance a child is born. Our balance is our love.

Man: Within the balance is the *procreant.* We, man and woman, are procreant *together.* We are only procreant with each other. Procreation is our eternal lineage. Our balance, as a procreant moment between two equal but opposite *sexed* forces, comprises the eternal.

Woman: The *First Pair* is always eternal. Our love that flows through our balance is eternal love. Our love always exists for our child. As it will never die; it sustains all life at all times.

Man: We, the F*irst Pair*, exist in the heart or soul of all things directing all things. Balance is our guide. Balance is our law. No one, not even us, can circumvent the *sexual balance* between a man and a woman.

Woman: Your anguish is that you seek and cannot find. Until you hold the balance of our love in your hearts, you can never find. When you do you will know that you *two* can never be lost for you, too, are the *First Pair,* knowing your own love together even before the beginning.

Man: I, man, divide the one.

Woman: I, woman, unite the two.

Man: We, dividing from and uniting with each other, *together* constitute the source of all creation. Not alone; not with something else. Not through anything else. Your life hinges on the *procreant balance* you hold with your eternal other half, just as does mine.

Woman: Don't despair. Rejoice. You, right now, can invite your eternal other half into your heart. I remember the day well when my husband and I said our prayer and took our vows together. That wonderful moment lives in our hearts to this day. We say our prayer and vows together each moment, every day. That is how it *lives.*

Man: Look at us, a man and a woman. What would you have us say? We stand not apart from you. We claim no dimension greater than you. We hold out our hands to you in the consciousness that we, the *First Pair*, can only shine the love to you that arises out of the love we have for our child.

Woman: My sisters, can you feel yourself holding your child in your arms, that child created by your husband and yourself? Is not that the greatest of all miracles?

Man: And brothers, feel the pride you have in securing your family. Every one of you, together with your wives, is surely the *First Pair*. May you take this stand for life.

Woman: The *First Pair* is the only stand my husband takes. And he gives this all to me. I receive all so that we, the *First Pair*, may be reproduced out of my spirit-womb once again. I am woman. All things born out of me come back into me to be reborn out of me.... For surely this is our truth.

Man: To woman I give my life. To woman I make my surrender. To woman I embrace my eternal life as man, only and always with her eternal life as woman. Together we, man and woman, stand on our life eternal.

Woman: How could it be any other way?

Man: The *First Pair*, an original idea, now being differentiated into consciousness as the source of all consciousness by a *First Pair*, is, from this moment on, delineated to be existent at the soul of all things, guiding all things to a universal awareness of 'itself' (as a two procreant forces/*First Pair*), an awareness that from this day forth can never be undone.

Woman: And there is love.

Memes, Bumper Stickers, Banner, and Flag

Memes, bumper stickers, banner, and flag are another way to get this word out. Below I give some examples.

We Will Always Be Together
We will always be together
Through sun and rain
Through time and pain
Together
Sharing our dreams along the way
In silence,
We, you and I
Man and Woman
Will always be together
Until eternity's end,
Listen, listen to our children
They say it is so.

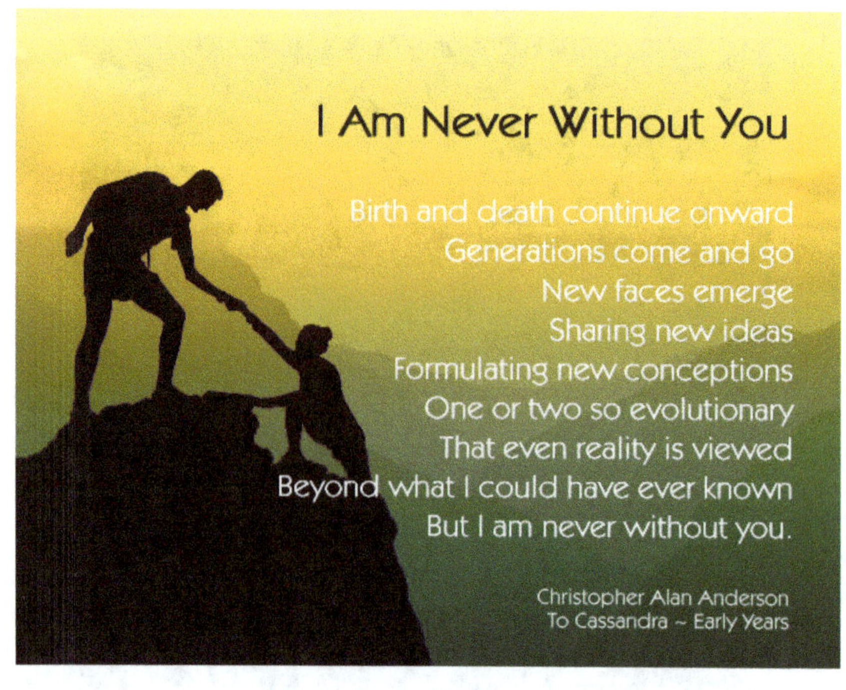
I Am Never Without You
Birth and death continue onward
Generations come and go
New faces emerge
Sharing new ideas
Formulating new conceptions
One or two so evolutionary
That even reality is viewed
Beyond what I could have ever known
But I am never without you.
Christopher Alan Anderson
To Cassandra ~ Early Years

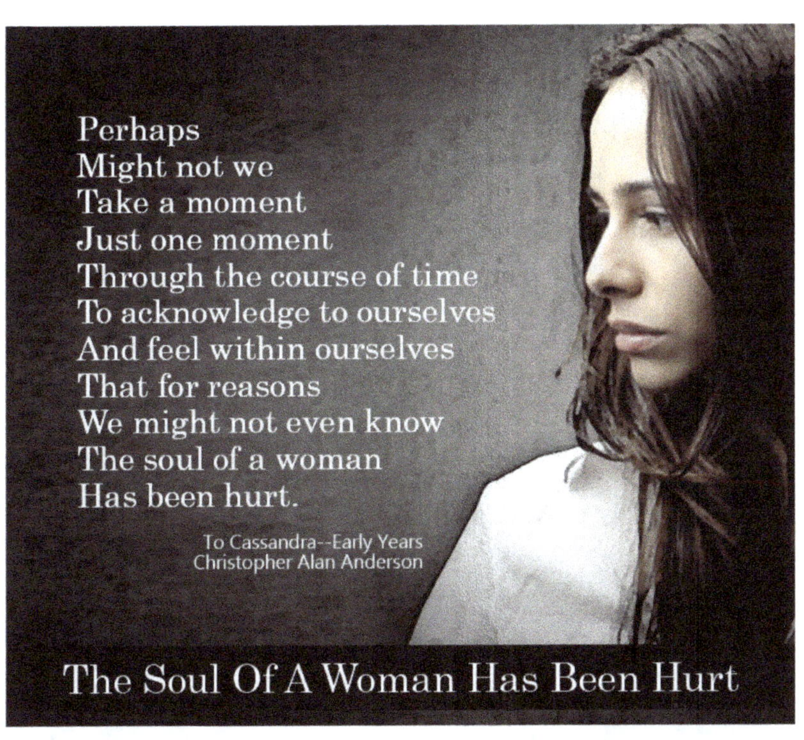
Perhaps
Might not we
Take a moment
Just one moment
Through the course of time
To acknowledge to ourselves
And feel within ourselves
That for reasons
We might not even know
The soul of a woman
Has been hurt.
To Cassandra--Early Years
Christopher Alan Anderson
The Soul Of A Woman Has Been Hurt

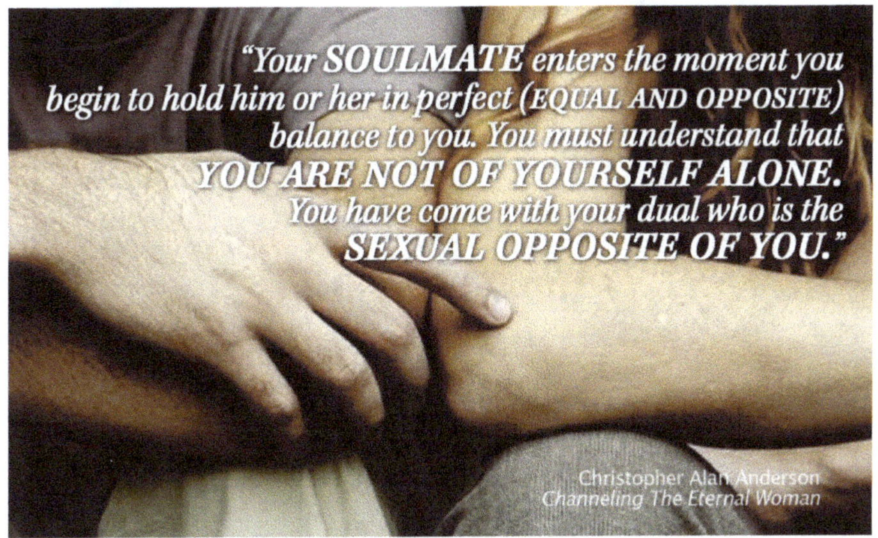
"Your SOULMATE enters the moment you
begin to hold him or her in perfect (EQUAL AND OPPOSITE)
balance to you. You must understand that
YOU ARE NOT OF YOURSELF ALONE.
You have come with your dual who is the
SEXUAL OPPOSITE OF YOU."
Christopher Alan Anderson
Channeling The Eternal Woman

I Am and You Are!

The Unity already is...

The forgiveness has taken place...

We have risen above...

Our prayer is answered...

We are love.

Christopher Alan Anderson
Meditation eCards

The Eternal and the PROCREATIVE are One

WWW.MANANDWOMANBALANCE.COM

MAN AND WOMAN BALANCE: WORLD-WIDE EVOLUTION

WWW.MANANDWOMANBALANCE.COM

Man and Woman Sovereignty

WWW.MANANDWOMANBALANCE.COM

MAN AND WOMAN
BALANCE
Equal & Opposite

Further Writings by Author

The Divine Touch: A New Creation for Life © 2021

When we understand the forces of male and female, we understand that both the division of the One and the unity of the Two are included. Both of them are primary. There just isn't anything above, prior to, or outside of the two sexual forces of creation. *Life is but procreation.*

Illumination: Joy in the Soul—The 2008-2009 Articles © 2010

So the spiritual component of energy, what we call "the light," is actually a moment of procreant love. In procreant love a man is giving his essence (his male light) to the woman and she is receiving it and giving to him her essence (female light). Equal and opposite, and so the universe moves or *procreates.* So often we make the mistake of just viewing procreation physically. *Procreation is the essential spiritual nature of the universe.* Each man and woman, in their giving to each other, are creating their eternal life *together.* Notice here that—*the procreant and the eternal are one.* When we understand this we have *joy.* We, man and woman, are giving to each other our life and our love. Today, I often hear people say that you can only love yourself or make yourself happy. This (singular) idea misses the whole point of relationship. A man does not love himself or make himself happy. He loves the woman and makes her happy. The same holds true for a woman. She loves her man and that makes him happy. We love and make another happy by giving these things—*which we already have.* Remember those ten two letter words: *If it is to be it is up to me.* Let's now change that to read: *If it is to be it is up to us.* We exist in a universe of us, not a universe of the singular "I" or the non-distinct "one," but an equal and opposite us. Let's let this *reality* be our joy and our love.

Spiritual Healing Through Eternal Love—The 2008-2009 Articles © 2010

The procreant (of man and woman balance) is then the dividing/uniting center/lineage of life. And so we see that the spiritual and the sexual go hand-in-hand, i.e., the eternal and the procreant are one. Who would have thought that the procreant creates the eternal—that in every birth of life there is eternal life?

And from this understanding we can now say—*we already love*, and we, man and woman, do so *primarily*. This suggests that a man already loves a woman and a woman already loves a man. *This love is primary to life*. It is primary to life because it is *procreant*. It is procreant because it (the two equal and opposite sexual forces) is held in perfect balance, dividing and uniting together. And so we now see that *the procreant interaction of a man and a woman is the love center of life eternal.*

The 2008-2009 Articles—The Coming of the Procreant Holy Spirit © 2010

The Holy Spirit is our connection to the eternal. It actually exists in each one of us. As Jesus said in John 14:18: *I will not leave you comfortless: I will come to you.* He is speaking of a spirit. Without this spirit we are not able to connect with the eternal. We don't even know what the eternal is or if there is an eternal. More and more people are calling themselves atheists today. They don't have a sense of the Holy Spirit within themselves. So we must ask, what is their inner compass? And it is not just atheists—what is the inner compass of the Christian, Jew, Muslim, Buddhist, Hindu, Secular Humanist, Homosexual, Environmentalist, Divine Feminist, etc., and why so many different ideas of what is the connective center or spirit of things? Jesus further says in John 14:26: *But the Comforter, which is the Holy Ghost, whom the Father will send in my name, he shall teach you all things, and bring all things to your remembrance, whatsoever I have said unto you.* But we haven't been taught all things and we do not remember (what is true). And so it appears, at least to me anyway, that the Holy Spirit actually has yet to arrive. This may be somewhat of a radical thought, especially to Christians, but is anything (spiritually) better today then it was thousands of years ago? Is man's (men and women) heart any different?

The 2008-2009 Articles—The Coming of the Procreant Holy Spirit © 2010

As we come to the end of this article, let's return to the title—*The Coming of the Procreant Holy Spirit.* This is the missing understanding, that this universe of ours is *procreant* in its nature. This is not a world created by "God," or saved by his "Son," etc. It is a procreant world of two equal and opposite forces, i.e., one man and one woman. Spiritually speaking we could say, *in the beginning*

Adam and Eve. Adam and Eve are the primaries. Every man represents Adam and every woman Eve. It is this joining together in the acknowledgment that *one is not without the other; both are needed for either to be* that is the Holy Spirit in our hearts. And so to bring the Holy Spirit into our hearts we must ask our eternal other half to come into our hearts. (Christians almost had it right in the asking of Jesus to come into their hearts. It is just that our savior is not Jesus but our eternal other half as we are equally the savior of our other half.) This asking our other half to come into our hearts is what I call *The Eternal Prayer.*

The Eternal Prayer
My blessed love,
please come into my heart
and live in me. Allow me, as well,
to come into your heart and live in you.
Let us, from this moment on,
live in each other's hearts,
our love together being our guide,
shining a light for all to see
that life is held simply
in "our" balance together.

The 2008-2009 Articles—Spiritual Procreation: Faith is the Substance © 2010

Both masculinism and feminism preclude us from entering into the *faith* that is *the substance of things hoped for, the evidence of things not seen.* Neither one of them can take us to a new metaphysical channel that we can now call *faith as procreant substance.* Only *spiritual procreation,* i.e., *procreant love,* i.e., *man and woman balance* can do that. Our faith is answered in the tangible, the real, the concrete substance of *spiritual procreation.* It is from *spiritual procreation* that we see the evidence. And what do we see? We see the *procreant love* we have with our *eternal other half* as it exists in our hearts right now reflected out into the world as the world at each and every moment. A new day has dawned.

Beauty © 2010; Meditations for Deepening Love © 2010

When I saw you for the first time, I knew my soul had been touched by beauty. I felt a light or radiance in the deepest part of me. How does one describe it? Is it just a feeling that cannot be put into words? Have you ever tried to define beauty? Let me say, everything, for the first time, began to make sense to me. Life had a coherency to it. Aristotle called beauty an organic unity. Maybe it is a divine harmony or an eternal consistency. In any event, my soul had been touched like never before. Like Dante after his vision of Beatrice, my life was never to be the same.

Reflections on Light: From a Homeless Shelter © 2021

Light is all substance. It is all energy. It is all consciousness. And it is also all life, i.e., sexual in its nature. Sexual implies desire which is force. It must divide into an equal and opposite sexual two (male and female). And, likewise, it must unite back into oneness (male-female)—*not a oneness outside of the sexual process but a oneness that is part and parcel of the sexual process.* And so, my friends, this is a vibratory universe, the two sexual forces dividing apart and uniting together in perfect procreant balance. And this is the whole enchilada. We can only know *Our Eternal Love* as the Source Light when we, male and female, are in our own sexual forms—reaching out to each other to **touch**.

Meditation As Spiritual Procreation © 2023

A touch also occurs in the purity of the heart. The touch, from one to another, is the miracle itself. It is a meeting from one pure heart to another. Jesus could not heal those who did not believe. They had to be open to his giving. They would have to be open in the pure heart for his giving to be received.

Spiritual healing is but the state of being **pure in heart**. Once the heart (also called the soul) is purified so can mental and physical healing take place. As earlier stated: *Light is the etheric substance. It is the light behind the light, i.e.,* ***Spiritual Light.*** *Ether/Light (**Spiritual Light**) is a Living substance.* Let us also add, it is a pure substance, pure in heart/soul. This is the key. We must begin our miracle/healing in the heart of the soul where the **touch** one unto another occurs. This touch is not just one-way, like from Jesus to you or me. It must run both ways.

Meditation As Spiritual Procreation © 2023

The **True Light** can only shine. It never fails to shine from one to another. It does not shine upon itself but upon another. And still we do not comprehend! How, may I ask, do we come to the Holy Spirit and the Eternal Birth when today darkness/disconnection hovers over us? What is that fundamental issue/imbalance that keeps us in bondage to this world?

Channeling the Eternal Woman © 2014

I, the Eternal Woman, stand as the counter-balance to the *Individual Man.* The Individual Man is that center-point of all men. A man's life purpose is to secure a woman. A woman's life purpose is to reproduce a man. Can that ever change? As such, a man can only find his rebirth, i.e., *eternal life* in me. Individual men have yet to understand this. And so they go about their "lives" creating "Gods" to believe in—which are nothing more than idols that they serve—that they may somehow reach eternal life. And then they enslave the women who are their eternal life connection. What folly. Any man who walks ahead of a woman in his life and heart cannot know life or love. We are co-creators together. We can only walk hand-in-hand.

That which you call belief systems, or might you call them philosophies or religions or enlightenments, or what you may call your sciences or any embodiments of thought, if they exclude man and woman as co-creators, they cannot be correct and true. I don't say this as somehow being superior to you. I say this in the frame of Individual Man and Eternal Woman together. Women have wept for thousands, no millions, of years for just a connection of *equality* between the Individual Man and the Eternal Woman. We are still weeping. Come to me my man and let me touch your heart and breathe new life into your soul. I call you from the space that you thought was somehow empty and have for so long been afraid to enter. But how can you fear me? I am the Eternal Woman. I can only give life to you as my love for you.

Meditation As Spiritual Procreation © 2023

Might I suggest, our Faith lieth in the **Holy Spirit,** the interconnective spirit of woman. This understanding is what brings man and woman together. **We together!** We, man and woman, TOGETHER, are the Way, the Truth, and the Life. We need to pluralize Genesis 1:27 from "...male and female created He them', to **Father and Mother procreated Son or Daughter**. We need to sexually pluralize all of our religions, East and West, not to mention our philosophies. A New Trinity—Sexual division and unification—stands as the Metaphysical Given. Such lies our faith <u>in life</u>.

The New Trinity © 1985; Selected Writings © 1988, 2010

The Holy Spirit

The Holy Spirit is our sense of our other half that resides in each one of us. We are all interconnected with our sexual other, dividing from and uniting with over and over. When in the divided or separate state, we are still intrinsically interconnected through our soul consciousness. Our sense of connection is our sense of spirit, our sense of life itself which is a sexual self-other creation. We might say that within each of us is the life-spirit or Holy Spirit of our sexual other, the balance of that being what we call God.

The Holy Spirit is with us at all times. Just as our loved one is always on our minds, so, too, is he or she always embedded in our hearts. That other serves as our motive force, our life impetus. One hasn't any meaning of himself or herself alone. One acts only and always as if acting towards that sexual other. That sexual other is that who we give to and receive from without which we have no reaction to our lives. The Holy Spirit is one's sexual other that resides in his or her heart at all times.

To accept the Holy Spirit into one's life is to accept that sexual other as one's other half and as equally necessary to one's existence. We have mislabeled this Holy Spirit as being of Jesus Christ or God but we are only speaking here of a conscious conversion to sexual self-other balance. It is this balance that purges one's soul of ignorance and envy and immerses one in the Holy Spirit of love.

The Divine Touch: A New Creation for Life © 2021

I, a man, who has come to speak the truth, have come to complete the message of Jesus so that we can understand the sexual nature of this procreative universe upon which **we**, man and woman, can become as One **together** than as Two...and One and as Two... BIRTH-LIFE-DEATH-REBIRTH, i.e., ETERNAL LIFE—and so then to overcome the world by simply **touching together** in this world. If I could perhaps touch your heart just as you have touched mine—and somehow convey to you: *There is just an Us, a We together*, certainly I would be most happy. Can't that be enough? Touching another's heart and receiving another's touch unto oneself must be enough. Let us not ask more of another or of ourselves.

The Light Behind the Light*

"I see a light no man or woman has ever seen. The unseen world is now the seen and known world; its order is beautiful, its balance perfect. Yes, I see a new world, the most Divine world that has ever come to pass. And I can even prove it to you, for, you see, I now see You."

***The Divine Touch: A New Creation for Life © 2021**

The Divine Touch: A New Creation for Life © 2021

Can you feel these words from the new construct of God the Father and God the Mother?; from God the Holy Son and God the Holy Daughter?; from God the living sexual spirit within you as male or as female—which ever sexuality you may be—always in connection with your equal and opposite other half? Within the Divine Trinity is the Divine Touch. Then you will walk the lands, hand-in-hand, as did Jesus and Mary Magdalene, shining the light of your sexual purity and rebirth for all to see. Then you will know that there cannot be male without female or female without male even if we are speaking of "God." Then you will know of your child abiding in the perfect balance of man and woman. And then you will know that every day is resurrection day; the rebirth of life within our sexual souls.

The Miracle of Life*

The miracle of life is that the whole of the universe/life is based on male and female procreant love without which there wouldn't be any universe/life!

***The Prime Movers: The Sovereignty of Man and Woman © 2015**

Meditation As Spiritual Procreation © 2023

Your love, at this precise moment, is a perfect love, as is mine. *And there is no fear in love.* (**1 John 4:18:** *There is no fear in love: but perfect love casteth out fear: because fear hath torment. He that feareth is not made perfect in love.*) Your love, as is mine, is a balanced love which is a perfect love. How can we know this? Because the Holy Trinity has been redefined to include, a priori, the female force of creation, to stand equal and opposite to the male force of creation. <u>This is the balance</u>. There is no other balance. And so <u>we together,</u>

male and female, walk the path of the Savior. Salvation is a dual encounter. It is A Love Perfected: The Coming Age of Spiritual Procreation. This understanding, this **Truth**, this **Courage**, this **Faith** comprises the <u>healing of our souls</u> as we now come into balance with one another. More specifically we come into sexual balance with our Eternal Other Half.

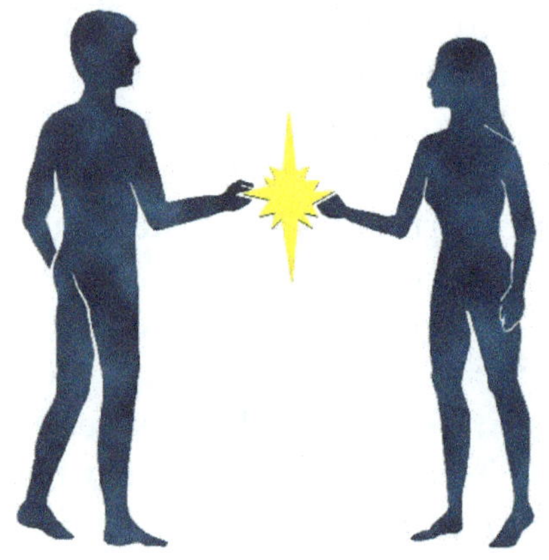

Action Plan

Man and Woman Balance is just a balance. It is not a religion, or even a belief system. It is just a real life, <u>sexual</u> balance, and, as such, it is a *direct touch*, man to woman and woman to man. There isn't any other or better world or reality out there. There is only this moment of Man and Woman Balance.

The Divine Touch: A New Creation for Life © 2021

The Divine Touch: A New Creation for Life © 2021

It, the Divine Touch, is brought to our awareness/life from the spiritual realm. Perhaps the only way to get there is through quieting the "dualistic mind"—what the mystics of all religions call meditation. (We might also call it a communion.) The spiritual only arises when the body and mind are still/balanced, i.e., transcended into the one light itself. To be with—being one with. But this light is not a singular "I Am" or a Universal (Capital S) "Self" or even a "sole Oneness" moment. It is not a (singular) Christ moment (or Jewish moment, Muslim moment, Hindu moment, etc.). It is not a "We the people" moment. It is not a "Black Lives (or White Lives) Matter" moment. It is not a LGBTPQ moment. No, it is only a <u>man, woman, and child</u> moment. This is to state it is an **alive moment** not a dead moment. And it is <u>alive</u> due to the two (equal and opposite) forces of creation. The light, or Divine Touch as I call it, is a living moment. Do you now see the paradigm shift taking place here? (The Divine Sacred Feminine returns to balance the Almighty Masculine. She should have never been lost.) And I will state: *"You will not survive without this one metaphysical step. Don't you know your religion is under attack—and with it the Constitutional basis of your beloved America (sovereignty in the people, unalienable rights of the people,* *and earning and owning by the people)—and, most importantly, the very fabric of your society, the two parent, male and female, family?"* Review *Family—The Force to Save the Planet.* Yes—

> **"Your soul is under attack. Don't you see it coming? The Marxist/LGBTPQ group is coming after you. They are out to destroy you and everything you stand for. You call on 'me' to save you. Yet, at the same time, you deny my essence. You deny me with your 501(c)(3) churches. You enslave yourself under the bondage of your IRS. You can no longer speak freely. You have sold out for the mega-church and its money while babies are left to die in abortion clinics—funded by taxpayer dollars, approved by your Congress! Some of you have become sanctuaries of homosexuality and pedophilia, and even worse, child sex trafficking and Occult worship and sacrifice. You approve of your (bankrupt/corporate) government bombing countries, killing thousands, no, hundreds of thousands of innocents, all to hide their counterfeit money scheme that you refuse to acknowledge. You don't know the enemy because you have become the enemy. You have already been conquered. Why? Because you committed the greatest of all sins. You placed your own personal salvation before another. You believed in 'me' only for your own personal salvation and, even worse, before your own love of another. Didn't you understand that the 'me' I spoke of was the universal 'Me' that did not and could not stand apart from the universal 'You.' I suppose I should have said, *"We <u>together</u> are the resurrection, and the life: anyone that believeth in Us, though he/she were dead, yet shall he/she live."* May you now understand, I did not come to die on the Cross for your sins nor resurrect in three days for your eternal life. I came to tell you that we must walk together—all as Children of Light? I stand neither**

above you nor below you. I can only stand with you. And so, allow me again to state, *"If you do not position the life process (Man and Woman Balance) as the metaphysical primary of life, you will never be able to defend life."*

Friends, wherever you are, whomever you may be, come forward at this time in our history and help close that fissure of unconsciousness that has been blocking us from a spiritual touch one unto another. It is just a conceptual shift, a small reconfiguration within our souls, a balancing/healing of our very eternal lives. Balance is the key, or may I say *sexual balance*. Sexual (procreant) balance (equal and opposite) sweeps away all of our previous imbalances and unlocks the door to an everlasting love. Everlasting love, also called Eternal Love, is the only healing we need, and only together can we be healed. Yes, you are now being called forward, invited, at this time, to take your place in the perfect balance that is Man and Woman Balance.

The Man and Woman Balance flag is the first flag that represents what may be called the balance of polar opposites, sexual sovereign pairs if you will, sovereign because that is the **balance,** what we may call the **Law of Love**. This is what the term Spiritual Procreation means; that each one of us is bequeathed with certain unalienable rights, among these are life, liberty, the pursuit of happiness, and allodial title, beginning with sound substance value/money, to that which we create/earn (give and receive). Not even our great founding Fathers could give us that. *We hold these truths to be self-evident....of the People, by the People, and for the People.* The American flag, which is linked to the American Declaration of Independence and Constitution of the united States of American, fell short. Its history is linked to the various bankruptcies of our Country from which the flag, for all purposes, was taken over by a foreign power. He who controls the currency controls the country, and the people, right? We have become chattel (:*an enslaved person held as the legal property of another*: from Merriam-Webster Dictionary) through our own Birth Certificates. There is an interesting and somewhat secret war going on right now over the American flag. You, the reader, might want to check out James Red Pills America—*Special OPS Revealed! Direst Secrets of the (DS) exposed! Whistleblower intel! Does Trump know?!* You can find it on Bitchute (1/22/23) and this confirms my own research from years ago. I suggest this because it just shows how important a flag is. And I certainly support the sanctity of the American flag. It signifies the stand of our sovereignty and unalienable rights; life, liberty, and the pursuit of happiness. No other flag had done that before. Let's not forget the 4th Amendment to the Constitution for the united States of America.

> **The Bill of Rights:**
> **Amendment IV to the Constitution**
> **as Ratified by the States on December 15, 1791**
>
> The right of the people to be secure in their persons, houses, papers, and effects, against unreasonable searches and seizures, shall not be violated, and no Warrants shall issue, but upon probable cause, supported by Oath or affirmation, and particularly describing the place to be searched, and the persons or things to be seized.

Brilliant! My point is that the American flag does not go far enough in that it does not cement itself in Man and Woman Balance which is the basis for the Sovereignty/Sanctity of Life. We must clearly understand that the Sovereignty/Sanctity of Life is only held together by the **Procreant Given of Man and Woman Balance**, i.e., **Spiritual Procreation**. The American flag does not enter this arena. This is why we are facing a collapse of our Country. Neither Christianity, Socialism, or LGBTQ, etc., can give to us that metaphysical foundation necessity to sustain life. Remember that beginning quote:

> On a personal note, when Mr. Anderson was asked to describe the writings and what he felt their message was he responded, "Spiritual procreation.

> Mankind has yet to distinguish the two sexes on the spiritual level. In this failure lies the root of our problems and why we cannot yet touch the eternal together. The message of Man and Woman Balance brings each of us together in love with our eternal other half right now."

The flag of Man and Woman Balance is the first flag that represents the **Sovereignty/Sanctity of Life** throughout the universe in that it represents our **spiritual healing**, the **healing of the hearts of man and woman through each other**. It is a universal construct that transcends all nations, or even planets.... And so you are being invited...please, if you will, contact the person or organization that gave you this invitation package so that you may take your place as a divine expression, gifting love in the sanctity of life (man, woman, and child) throughout the universe.

And lastly, please feel free to send this Invitation Package to whomever you think might treasure it. This, **Man and Woman Balance**, is the paradigm shift that is itself the *Miracle of Life*. Thank you for your time and patience.

www.manandwomanbalance.com

To Cassandra—Early Years © 1985, 1994

Touch

At times
At times in this universe
We come upon each other
And touch
Briefly,
Or for a longer spell
Lightly,
Or only we can tell
We touch
Male and female
Each touch
Securing and reproducing
A complete touch,
And all we really know
Is the love
Between ourselves
And our other half.

Man and woman
Live
And struggle
And walk and rest
And die and concentrate
And hope and exaggerate
And despair and recreate
Only, only
Always together.

Cassandra,
Shall you and I
Walk into our silence
Together
Down the aisle
Arm and arm
Into the abyss
Forever
Only to return
When called by desire
Between a man and a woman
To touch.

Requesting Assistance in Production, Promotion, & Distribution

This, the **Message of Man and Woman Balance**, is a world-wide endeavor. It is for every Man and Woman—to come together in spiritual procreation for the very survival of Humanity. Humanity begins in Family and Family can no longer be held down, redefined, and broken. Family—Man, Woman, and Child—is the **Sovereign**. I, myself, have been working on this message for some 50 years—essentially alone. May another... and then another... come to assist. Assistance is being requested for website, printing, promotion, and distribution. There is a Humanitarian Project link at www.manandwomanbalance.com where one may donate/gift if so moved. Also, one may offer assistance with social media production, promotion, and support. Thank you.

Contact Information:
contact@manandwomanbalance.com
www.manandwomanbalance.com

Author: Christopher Alan Anderson (1950-) received the basis of his education from the University of Science and Philosophy, Swannanoa, Waynesboro, Virginia. He resides in the transcendental/romantic tradition, that vein of spiritual creativity of the philosopher and poet. His quest has been to define and express an eternal *romantic* reality from which a man and a woman could *together* stand and create a *living* universe. Mr. Anderson began these writings in 1971. The first writings were published in 1985.

Writings by the Author:

The Divine Touch: A New Creation for Life!
Humanitarian Project: Man and Woman Balance
Etheric Materialization Into Form!
Selected Writings—Volume 3: A New Trinity
Meditation as Spiritual Procreation
Let There Be Life!
The Man and Woman Manifesto: What We Believe!
Channeling the Eternal Woman
The Case Against Man and Woman – A Philosophy on Trial
Meditations for Deepening Love
Spiritual Healing of Our Eternal Souls for All Time
The Prime Movers: The Sovereignty of Man and Woman
Reflections on Light: From a Homeless Shelter
The Metaphysics of Sex ...in a Changing World!
Wealth Plus+ Empowering Your Everyday!
To Cassandra—Early Years
The 2008 - 2009 Articles

Man, Woman, and God

The Man and Woman Relationship: A New Center for the Universe

Illumination

Selected Writings—Volume 2

The Discovery of Life

The Man and Woman Manifesto: Let the Revolution Begin

Psychotherapy As If Life Really Mattered

The Universal Religion: The Final Destiny of Mankind

The Truth Revealed: My Answer to the World

Healing In The Light & The Art and Practice of Creativity

Selected Writings

For ordering information go to:

www.manandwomanbalance.com

Comments from Facebook

July 11, 2017

Dawn M. Dawset (UK): A well over due awakening. My conceptual consciousness has often naturally thought upon these lines of teachings, a huge subject of truth to me. I'm inspired by your work. It's definitely a ground breaking read. Thank you.

www.ingramcontent.com/pod-product-compliance
Lightning Source LLC
LaVergne TN
LVHW021134080426
835509LV00010B/1350

* 9 7 8 1 5 0 6 9 1 5 3 7 1 *